JBoss Weld CDI for Java Platform

Learn CDI concepts and develop modern
web applications using JBoss Weld

Ken Finnigan

[PACKT] open source*
PUBLISHING   community experience distilled

BIRMINGHAM - MUMBAI

JBoss Weld CDI for Java Platform

First published: July 2013

Production Reference: 1050713

Published by Packt Publishing Ltd.
Livery Place
35 Livery Street
Birmingham B3 2PB, UK.

ISBN 978-1-78216-018-2

www.packtpub.com

Cover Image by Timappa Shetty (sparkling.spectrum.123@gmail.com)

Credits

Author

Ken Finnigan

Reviewer

George Gastaldi

Acquisition Editor

Usha Iyer

Commissioning Editor

Llewellyn F. Rozario

Meeta Rajani

Technical Editors

Sampreshita Maheshwari

Veena Pagare

Copy Editors

Aditya Nair

Alfida Paiva

Laxmi Subramanian

Project Coordinator

Michelle Quadros

Proofreader

Maria Gould

Indexer

Priya Subramani

Production Coordinator

Aditi Gajjar

Cover Work

Aditi Gajjar

About the Author

Ken Finnigan is a Senior Software Engineer at Red Hat, technical lead of the JBoss Portlet Bridge project, a member of the GateIn development team, and the founder of the Arquillian Portal Extension. As a consultant and engineer he has over 15 years development experience with enterprises throughout the world using technologies that include Java EE frameworks (JSF, CDI, EJB3, Hibernate, and Seam), Java testing frameworks (Arquillian, JUnit, and TestNG), Maven, Ant, and a variety of others. In his spare time, he is a committer for Apache DeltaSpike, ShrinkWrap, and Arquillian. He is also the author of *GateIn Cookbook*, *Packt Publishing*.

I'd like to thank my wonderful wife, Erin, and my family for all their support and understanding through the entire book development process. I'd also like to thank George Gastaldi for agreeing to review the book.

About the Reviewer

George Gastaldi is a Senior Software Engineer from Brazil working at RedHat, notably as a core developer for the JBoss Forge project. He is also the leader of Seam 3 Reports and the co-leader of the Seam 3 JCR module. George has been working professionally with Java since 2000. In 2006, George joined Apache as an individual committer to work on Apache ServiceMix (an open source JBI-compliant ESB). George is a JCP individual member and also a member of the CDI 1.1 spec team. He also promotes Java technology by giving speeches at Brazilian conferences, such as JUDCon Brazil 2013 and The Developer's Conference 2012.

I wish to thank my wife Estéfany de Souza Gastaldi for supporting me during long nights, my parents Gilberto and Noeli Gastaldi, my sister Alessandra, and God for giving me the needed strength and faith.

www.PacktPub.com

Support files, eBooks, discount offers and more

You might want to visit www.PacktPub.com for support files and downloads related to your book.

Did you know that Packt offers eBook versions of every book published, with PDF and ePub files available? You can upgrade to the eBook version at www.PacktPub.com and as a print book customer, you are entitled to a discount on the eBook copy. Get in touch with us at service@packtpub.com for more details.

At www.PacktPub.com, you can also read a collection of free technical articles, sign up for a range of free newsletters and receive exclusive discounts and offers on Packt books and eBooks.

http://PacktLib.PacktPub.com

Do you need instant solutions to your IT questions? PacktLib is Packt's online digital book library. Here, you can access, read and search across Packt's entire library of books.

Why Subscribe?

- Fully searchable across every book published by Packt
- Copy and paste, print and bookmark content
- On demand and accessible via web browser

Free Access for Packt account holders

If you have an account with Packt at www.PacktPub.com, you can use this to access PacktLib today and view nine entirely free books. Simply use your login credentials for immediate access.

Table of Contents

Preface

The CDI specification standardized the process of dependency injection for Java EE, opening the door to efficient integration with components and frameworks for your applications. JBoss Weld is the open source reference implementation for CDI that simplifies the development of applications with dependency injection.

JBoss Weld CDI for Java Platform will explain dependency injection with JBoss Weld and how you can use it to ensure that your applications take advantage of type safety, making your applications easier to debug and maintain. It is filled with information on what scopes CDI provides for your applications, how to fire and listen to events, creating new beans with producers, interceptors, and decorators, and developing portable extensions.

JBoss Weld CDI for Java Platform will have you up and running with CDI on JBoss Weld in a short space of time. Once we've covered the main topics of CDI, we will develop a simple application using CDI services with REST endpoints that we connect to from JSF and AngularJS.

What this book covers

Chapter 1, What is a Bean?, provides an overview of CDI beans and their history, before explaining how a Java class can be a bean.

Chapter 2, Dependency Injection and Lookup, explains injection and lookup functions, by understanding qualifiers and injection points. We also cover some possible Weld dependency errors and how our beans are proxied.

Chapter 3, Deploying JBoss Weld, covers how to deploy JBoss Weld to JBoss AS, GlassFish, and Tomcat.

Chapter 4, Scopes and Contexts, explains the scopes that are provided by CDI and how they should be used. We also explain pseudo scopes and creating a custom scope.

Chapter 5, Producers, covers producer methods and fields, injecting into producer methods, and how we can clean up beans that we produce.

Chapter 6, Interceptors and Decorators, explains how to create and enable an interceptor, and how their bindings are defined. We also look at enabling decorators and what is a decorator delegate.

Chapter 7, Events, explains how to listen for and fire events, and what type of payload can be sent. We also explain advanced event qualifiers and how to listen for events during specific transaction phases.

Chapter 8, Writing a Portable Extension, explains how to create an extension to CDI and what events the container fires that we can utilize. We then cover some examples of what can be achieved within an extension.

Chapter 9, Book Store – CDI Services, covers the development of CDI services, REST endpoints, and communicating with a database for our example application.

Chapter 10, Book Store – User Interfaces, explains how to develop a JSF admin interface and a user interface using AngularJS for our example application that will interact with our services.

What you need for this book

To be able to run the examples from this book, you should have:

- Any operating system based on Linux, Mac OS X, or Windows
- **Java Development Kit (JDK)** 1.6 or 1.7
- Apache Maven (latest version)
- JBoss Weld (latest 1.x version)
- Your favorite runtime container: JBoss AS7, GlassFish, or Apache Tomcat

Who this book is for

This book is for anyone wanting to understand what CDI 1.0 is and how it can be used to benefit an application's architecture. Experience with Java is required, but only so far as is needed to understand the coding constructs of the language. RESTful architecture, AngularJS, and **Java Server Faces (JSF)** skills are suggested, though not essential.

Conventions

In this book, you will find a number of styles of text that distinguish between different kinds of information. Here are some examples of these styles, and an explanation of their meaning.

Code words in text are shown as follows: "In the preceding examples we specified @RequestScoped."

A block of code is set as follows:

```
@RequestScoped
public class MySecondBean {
  MyFirstBean firstBean;
  @Inject
  public MySecondBean(MyFirstBean firstBean) {
    this.firstBean = firstBean;
  }
}
```

New terms and **important words** are shown in bold. Words that you see on the screen, in menus or dialog boxes for example, appear in the text like this: "clicking the **Next** button moves you to the next screen".

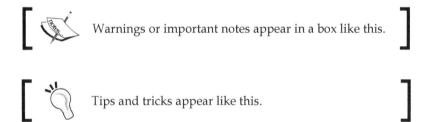

Warnings or important notes appear in a box like this.

Tips and tricks appear like this.

Reader feedback

Feedback from our readers is always welcome. Let us know what you think about this book—what you liked or may have disliked. Reader feedback is important for us to develop titles that you really get the most out of.

To send us general feedback, simply send an e-mail to feedback@packtpub.com, and mention the book title via the subject of your message.

If there is a topic that you have expertise in and you are interested in either writing or contributing to a book, see our author guide on www.packtpub.com/authors.

Customer support

Now that you are the proud owner of a Packt book, we have a number of things to help you to get the most from your purchase.

Downloading the example code

You can download the example code files for all Packt books you have purchased from your account at http://www.packtpub.com. If you purchased this book elsewhere, you can visit http://www.packtpub.com/support and register to have the files e-mailed directly to you.

Errata

Although we have taken every care to ensure the accuracy of our content, mistakes do happen. If you find a mistake in one of our books—maybe a mistake in the text or the code—we would be grateful if you would report this to us. By doing so, you can save other readers from frustration and help us improve subsequent versions of this book. If you find any errata, please report them by visiting http://www.packtpub.com/submit-errata, selecting your book, clicking on the **errata submission form** link, and entering the details of your errata. Once your errata are verified, your submission will be accepted and the errata will be uploaded on our website, or added to any list of existing errata, under the Errata section of that title. Any existing errata can be viewed by selecting your title from http://www.packtpub.com/support.

Piracy

Piracy of copyright material on the Internet is an ongoing problem across all media. At Packt, we take the protection of our copyright and licenses very seriously. If you come across any illegal copies of our works, in any form, on the Internet, please provide us with the location address or website name immediately so that we can pursue a remedy.

Please contact us at copyright@packtpub.com with a link to the suspected pirated material.

We appreciate your help in protecting our authors, and our ability to bring you valuable content.

Questions

You can contact us at questions@packtpub.com if you are having a problem with any aspect of the book, and we will do our best to address it.

1
What is a Bean?

This chapter will introduce us to beans and their history prior to **Contexts and Dependency Injection** (**CDI**) becoming a part of **Java Enterprise Edition** (**Java EE**). After a short history, we will define what a bean is and what characteristics and behavior a Java class requires to be considered a bean.

 JSR-299: Contexts and Dependency Injection for the Java EE platform was finalized in December 2009. CDI 1.1 is due to be released in the first half of 2013 to coincide with the release of Java EE 7.

The history of beans

Beans have been used to refer to many different kinds of Java classes over the years. The oldest use of a bean is from 1996, when Sun introduced JavaBeans as a term for a reusable software component for Java that defined a series of rules as to how a Java class should be developed. Those original rules have become ubiquitous to the point that the term JavaBeans is rarely, if ever, used anymore.

Since that initial use of the bean in 1996, there have been many uses of the term in third-party frameworks such as Seam and Spring. The term was also used in EE specifications for **Enterprise JavaBeans** (**EJBs**) and **Java Server Faces** (**JSF**) where they were called **Managed Beans**. Even though the term "bean" had been used by various specifications within the Java EE platform, there was never a consistent or clear definition of what a bean is made of and how it could be utilized.

With the release of Java EE 6 in December 2009, for the first time the Managed Bean specification brought a common standard and definition of a bean to the entire Java EE platform. This definition was expanded upon within the EJB and CDI companion specifications of Java EE 6 and will continue to be utilized as more EE specifications continue to adopt the definition of a managed bean.

Definition of a bean

A bean is simply a **Plain Old Java Object** (**POJO**) that is managed by a container instead of an application. With this simple definition of a bean, most of your existing Java classes can be utilized as beans with minimal to no changes, such as adding annotations.

```
public class MyFirstBean {
}
```

It may not look like much, but the preceding Java class is all that is required for the most basic of CDI beans, which use the @Dependent scope (see *Chapter 4, Scopes and Contexts*).

To specify a CDI scope other than @Dependent, the bean will need a means for **Weld** to generate a Proxy (see *Chapter 2, Dependency Injection and Lookup*) of the bean for injection. For a bean to be able to be proxied by the container, it needs a non-private constructor with no parameters, commonly referred to by Java developers as a default constructor. Our bean is now:

```
@RequestScoped
public class MyFirstBean {
  public MyFirstBean() {
  }
}
```

It is also possible for a bean to be proxied by the container if it does not have a constructor with any parameters, but it does require a constructor to be annotated with @Inject, such as the following:

```
@RequestScoped
public class MySecondBean {
  MyFirstBean firstBean;

  @Inject
  public MySecondBean(MyFirstBean firstBean) {
    this.firstBean = firstBean;
  }
}
```

In the preceding examples we specified @RequestScoped, but we could also have chosen @ApplicationScoped, @SessionScoped, or @ConversationScoped.

 For complete details on the various scopes that are provided by CDI, see *Chapter 4, Scopes and Contexts*.

Any object that is bound to a lifecycle context is a bean, which enables CDI to provide support for Java EE Managed Beans and EJB Session Beans. Due to this inherent support in CDI, EJB Session Beans and Managed Beans can inject other beans into them as well as be injected into POJOs that are also beans.

When creating a CDI bean, we need to be concerned only with specifying the type and functionality of any beans that our bean will depend on to complete its work. This frees both the developer and the bean from being concerned with the following:

- The lifecycle of the bean being injected, and how that differs from the lifecycle of the bean that requested it

- Whether the type defined is a concrete implementation or an interface, and how the implementation for injection is to be created or retrieved

- If other beans also inject the same bean, how it should be handled to prevent a deadlock

This loose coupling between a bean and any beans that it depends on not only simplifies the development process, but also supports different use cases through alteration of which concrete implementation is being chosen at runtime, how the bean lifecycle will operate, and which threading model a bean utilizes.

With loose coupling, we could provide an `@Alternative` (see *Chapter 2, Dependency Injection and Lookup*) implementation of a credit card provider for use in development and testing environments to prevent spurious credit card payments being triggered, with the implementation that communicates with the credit card provider used only in production.

Is my class a bean?

For almost every Java class that we as developers have ever written, the answer would be yes, most definitely, as long as the Java class has either a constructor with no parameters or a constructor that is annotated with `@Inject`.

There is only one requirement that CDI mandates for a Java class to be injected as a bean, and that's for the Java class to be packaged into an appropriate archive (such as a JAR or WAR) that contains a descriptor file called `beans.xml`. This descriptor file needs to be present in the `META-INF` folder of a JAR or the `WEB-INF` folder of a WAR.

It's perfectly fine for `beans.xml` to be completely empty or only contain the following XML content:

```
<beans xmlns="http://java.sun.com/xml/ns/javaee"
  xmlns:xsi="http://www.w3.org/2001/XMLSchema-instance"
  xsi:schemaLocation="
```

```
        http://java.sun.com/xml/ns/javaee
        http://java.sun.com/xml/ns/javaee/beans_1_0.xsd">
</beans>
```

For most applications, the sole purpose of `beans.xml` is to notify CDI that there are beans within the archive that need to be scanned, so that they are available to have beans injected into them as well as be injected into other beans that may not be present within this archive.

What does it mean to be a bean?

According to the CDI specification:

A bean comprises the following attributes:

- *A (non-empty) set of bean types*
- *A (non-empty) set of qualifiers*
- *A scope*
- *Optionally, a bean EL name*
- *A set of interceptor bindings*
- *A bean implementation*

Furthermore, a bean may or may not be an alternative.

Bean types

In most cases, beans acquire references to other beans through dependency injection. The point at which a bean is injected will specify the type of that bean and a set of qualifiers. With the help of the bean type and qualifiers, Weld determines the implementation of a bean to provide for injection.

A bean type can be a class or interface that is visible to clients that wish to inject it. For instance, an EJB Session Bean implementation is not visible to clients, but its `@Local` interface is visible.

 EJB remote interfaces are not bean types of a Session Bean, and therefore they cannot be injected directly. They must be injected by defining a resource.

```
public class CandyStore extends CommonStore
implements Store<Candy> {
   ...
}
```

In this Java class, there are four bean types defined: `CandyStore`, `CommonStore`, `Store<Candy>`, and the implicit type `java.lang.Object`. An interesting point to note is that a parameterized type is considered a bean type by CDI, but only if it contains an actual type parameter and not a wildcard.

We are able to restrict which bean types are valid for any given Java class with the `@Typed` annotation by providing a defined set of bean types that can be accepted. We can restrict the types from the previous example to only `Store<Candy>` and the implicit `java.lang.Object` type, with the following:

```
@Typed(Store.class)
public class CandyStore extends CommonStore
implements Store<Candy> {
   ...
}
```

Qualifiers

A qualifier allows us to disambiguate a type without the need to leave type-safety and revert to string-based names, which we all know are fodder for runtime errors. All we need for defining a qualifier is to create an annotation that is annotated with `@Qualifier`.

```
@Qualifier
@Target ( { TYPE, METHOD, PARAMETER, FIELD } )
@Retention ( RUNTIME )
public @interface User {}
```

Here, we've defined a qualifier called `User`. Specifying `RUNTIME` retention informs the Java VM that we want the annotation information recorded in the class file of any bean that specifies this qualifier, so that it may be read at runtime. The values of `TYPE`, `METHOD`, `PARAMETER`, and `FIELD` specify valid locations within a bean where the qualifier may be placed.

 The `@Retention` values are found in `java.lang.annotation.RetentionPolicy` and the `@Target` values are found in `java.lang.annotation.ElementType`.

With our qualifier annotation, we are now able to disambiguate an injection point. The following injection point has a bean type of `Account` and a qualifier of `@User`:

```
@Inject
@User
Account userAccount;
```

The Weld container searches for a bean that matches the same bean type and all the qualifiers and each injection point that has been defined. If Weld doesn't find exactly one match, an error is reported during startup that there is an ambiguous injection point, which is Weld's way of telling you that there are too many beans that match the bean type and qualifiers.

To inform Weld that a bean has a specific qualifier, we annotate the bean class with it. The following bean would match the injection point from the previous code snippet:

```
@User
public class UserAccount implements Account {
    ...
}
```

 Any bean or injection point that does not explicitly specify a qualifier will have the default qualifier `@Default` assigned to it.

Scope

In the previous examples, we've utilized the CDI scopes that are provided for us, but what is a scope? A scope is the means by which a bean specifies its lifecycle and the visibility of its instances.

For instance, `@SessionScoped` binds a bean to a user session and is shared across all requests that execute in the context of that session.

 Once a bean is bound to its context, it cannot be removed from that context. The bean will remain in that context until the time the context is destroyed by the container. It's especially important to keep this in mind when developing beans that will hold large amounts of data and for how long that data needs to be retained.

Expression Language (EL)

A bean can be referenced from non-Java code if it supports Unified EL expressions, such as with JSF and JSP pages, but it requires an EL name to be defined.

The `@Named` annotation specifies the EL name for a bean, as follows:

```
@Named("book")
public class HistoryBook implements Serializable {
    ...
}
```

We can now access the bean in a JSF page:

```
<h:outputText value="#{book.isbn}" />
```

If we aren't particular about what EL name a bean is given, we can specify `@Named` without any value and it will default to the unqualified class name, with the first character converted to lower case. In the previous example, this would give us an EL name of `historyBook`.

Alternatives

If we need to vary which implementation is chosen depending on the deployment environment or some other factor, we can create an alternative bean that can be activated when needed.

For instance, if we want to create a mock or dummy implementation that is only used in testing environments, we can write the following:

```
@Alternative
public class DummyLogger extends LoggerImpl {
    ...
}
```

It's general practice to only annotate a bean with `@Alternative` when there is at least one other implementation of an interface it implements or any of its bean types, otherwise there wouldn't be anything for it to be an alternative of.

Alternatives are chosen by selecting an alternative in the CDI descriptor file, `beans.xml`, of the JAR or WAR that uses it.

This topic will be covered in greater detail in *Chapter 2, Dependency Injection and Lookup*.

Which classes are beans?

We're going to explore the different kinds of beans that Weld supports without any work on our part.

Managed Beans

As mentioned earlier, the Managed Beans specification was introduced in Java EE 6 to provide a common definition of a Managed Bean. All that's required to create a Managed Bean is to annotate it with @ManagedBean, though CDI doesn't require us to do so.

 JSF also has a @ManagedBean annotation to define their beans, and it's important to not confuse the two as they are separate annotations. Future releases of the JSF specification will endeavor to close this gap by utilizing the annotation from the Managed Beans specification.

Earlier in this chapter, we covered the requirements for constructors of a Java class to be a Managed Bean, but the CDI specification states that it must also meet the following conditions:

- *It is not a non-static inner class*
- *It is a concrete class or is annotated* @Decorator
- *It is not annotated with an EJB component-defining annotation or declared as an EJB bean class in* ejb-jar.xml
- *It does not implement* javax.enterprise.inject.spi.Extension

According to the preceding conditions, **Java Persistence API (JPA)** entities are also Managed Beans! Trying to use entities as Managed Beans will cause runtime issues when attempting to persist Managed Beans that have been proxied by CDI.

 We recommend to not directly inject an entity class into your beans, and they should not be assigned a scope other than @Dependent.

Session Beans

Session Beans can take advantage of CDI just like any other bean, though there are a few restrictions due to Session Beans having their lifecycle managed separate to CDI.

Message-driven and entity beans are not contextual objects in the CDI sense, so they are not able to be injected into other beans. It is possible to inject beans into a message-driven bean, and use interceptors and decorators to utilize some of the CDI functionalities that are available.

As the EJB container controls the lifecycle of a stateless Session Bean and a singleton Session Bean, there is no need to specify any CDI scope for these, but a stateful Session Bean may use any scope it requires.

Producers

In these final two sections, we will introduce producers, both method and field, which can be used to provide a CDI bean that isn't a Java class, per se. Producers are often useful in a situation where it is not known during development which particular qualified bean instance needs to be used, and producers allow us to create a bean that depends on runtime information for its creation.

Producers provide a source for new bean instances. A producer will be invoked by Weld when there is no instance of that bean in the required context.

We will cover producers in detail in *Chapter 5, Producers*.

Producer methods

To create a producer on a method, all that's required is to annotate the method with @Produces, along with any other qualifiers that we want the bean being produced to fulfill.

 Though producer methods can be called by our application, just as any other method, the returned bean will be completely outside the control of CDI. If the method has parameters, they will not be injected with beans at all; they would need to be passed just like any method call.

We'll define a producer method for UserAccount from an earlier example:

```
public class AccountManager {
  @Produces
  @User
  Account getUserAccount() {
    . . .
  }
}
```

The bean created from this producer can then be injected by using:

```
@Inject
@User
Account userAccount;
```

We can also add `@Named` to allow the bean to be accessed via EL, which for this example would be `userAccount`.

Producer methods can also declare parameters, and the container will retrieve a bean that matches the bean type and qualifiers that can be passed into the method.

Producer fields

Producer fields are a simpler alternative to producer methods, as they remove the need to create a method and thus reduce boilerplate code. If we converted the producer method from the previous example, it would be as follows:

```
public class AccountManager {
  @Produces
  @User
  Account userAccount = ...;
}
```

In situations where you have a bean with a field that you want to make available to other beans, using a producer field is often the best way to achieve this as it only involves one or more annotations being added to the existing field definition.

We can also add `@Named` to the producer field and access the bean with the same EL name from the previous example.

Summary

We covered a lot of information in this chapter about CDI concepts around what a bean is, such as qualifiers, scopes, alternatives, and producers. It's a lot to comprehend in one go, particularly if dependency injection is not a concept that is familiar.

As we progress through the following chapters, each concept that we've discussed here will become clearer as we delve into further details and provide more examples.

2

Dependency Injection and Lookup

In this chapter, we will delve into the details of typesafe dependency injection, qualifiers, alternatives, client proxies, as well as provide insight into the rules that Weld uses to determine which bean to provide for each injection point. We'll finish up with how to programmatically retrieve beans directly from your application.

What is an injection point?

An injection point is identified by the `@Inject` annotation. Previously, we covered a nondefault constructor for a bean that was annotated with `@Inject`, as shown in the following code:

```
public class PaymentProcessor {
  private final Payment payment;

  @Inject
  public PaymentProcessor(Payment payment) {
    this.payment = payment;
  }
}
```

This is known as bean constructor parameter injection and there can only be one constructor annotated with `@Inject` in a bean.

If a single constructor that defines every bean that we need to use, and thus needs to be injected, is not favored, there are two other ways to inject into our bean:

1. Create a bean that utilizes initializer method parameter injection, which has no restrictions on how many methods may be annotated with `@Inject`. If we were to change the `PaymentProcessor` class to use initializer method parameter injection, it would look like the following code snippet:

    ```
    public class PaymentProcessor {
      private final Payment payment;

      @Inject
      void setPayment(Payment payment) {
        this.payment = payment;
      }
    }
    ```

2. Create a bean that utilizes direct field injection, which also has no restrictions on the number of fields in a bean that have `@Inject` present. `PaymentProcessor` would now be:

    ```
    public class PaymentProcessor {
      @Inject
      private Payment payment;
    }
    ```

The major advantage of field over method injection is that it doesn't require any getter or setter methods to be present on the bean to perform the injection.

 To create beans that are immutable, the best approach for a bean is to use either constructor or field injection.

The first time that a bean is instantiated by the container is the point when beans that match the injection points are injected ready for use.

The order in which a bean is constructed by the container is as follows:

1. Call the constructor of the bean to create an instance of the bean; this can either be the default constructor or one marked `@Inject`.
2. All fields of the bean marked `@Inject` will have their values initialized.
3. All initializer methods on the bean are called.
4. If a `@PostConstruct` method is present, it is called.

The order in which initializer methods are called by the container is not defined by the CDI spec. Depending on the order in which they are called is not recommended as each implementation can use a different ordering.

There are three types of injection points that don't require the presence of `@Inject`: `producer`, `observer`, and `disposer` methods.

```
@Produces
PaymentProcessor createProcessor(Payment payment) {
  return new PaymentProcessor(payment);
}
```

We'll cover observer methods as part of *Chapter 7, Events*.

Typesafe resolution

The CDI specification defines the process of matching a bean to an injection point as **typesafe resolution**. Bean type and qualifiers are the criterion used by the container to perform typesafe resolution for an application.

The process of typesafe resolution is usually performed by the container during application startup, making it possible for the container to end the startup process and warn the user if any beans have unsatisfied or unresolved ambiguous dependencies.

For a bean to be assignable to a given injection point, we need to make sure that:

- Its bean type matches the bean type of the injection point.
- It has all qualifiers that were specified on the injection point, and any member values of those qualifiers have the same value if the member is not annotated with `@Nonbinding` (we cover this in the next section). If no qualifiers are present on an injection point, `@Default` is assumed by the container.

 For the purpose of matching a bean type, a primitive type will match its corresponding wrapper type in `java.lang` and array types will match if their element types match.

The typesafe resolution process is designed in such a way that it allows more than one bean to implement the same bean type. This provides great flexibility to us by:

- The injection point selecting a specific implementation of a bean type through one or more qualifiers
- A deployment process selecting a specific implementation for a given deployment scenario, without application changes, by enabling or disabling an alternative through XML configuration
- Allowing beans to be divided into separate modules

Typically, when we begin developing a new application we will only have a single bean of each bean type we define. As we develop our application it becomes common place, and often necessary, to introduce various implementations for a bean type to satisfy the requirements of different runtime scenarios.

Qualifiers

A qualifier is an annotation that has `@Qualifier` declared on it, which signifies to the container that this qualifier annotation can be utilized on injection points and beans to distinguish different implementations of the same bean type.

A qualifier annotation, without any members, is just:

```
@Qualifier
@Retention(RUNTIME)
@Target( { TYPE, METHOD, FIELD, PARAMETER } )
public @interface MyQualifier {}
```

 @MyQualifier has been defined for use on a Java type, method, field, or method parameter.

We can use field injection with `@MyQualifier` by:

```
@Inject
@MyQualifier
private Locale myLocale;
```

Or constructor injection:

```
@Inject
public Notifications(@MyQualifier Locale myLocale) {
  this.myLocale = myLocale;
}
```

Or an initializer method:

```
@Inject
public void setLocale(@MyQualifier Locale myLocale {
  this.myLocale = myLocale;
}
```

Lastly, producing a `Locale` with the `@MyQualifier` annotation to match the injection points:

```
@Produces
@MyQualifier
public Locale getMyLocale() {
  return Locale.US;
}
```

@Default and @Any

As we've mentioned previously, for any injection point that does not explicitly declare a qualifier annotation, the container will assume the presence of `@Default`, referred to as the default qualifier. The default qualifier is also assumed for any bean that does not declare one. If a bean contains the `@Named` annotation, it is still assumed to have `@Default` as `@Named` is not a qualifier annotation.

As the default qualifier is assumed to be present, both the beans in the following code are equivalent:

```
@Default
public class Ticket { ... }

public class Ticket { ... }
```

All beans of an application are given the `@Any` qualifier, whether or not there are other qualifier annotations specified. In our preceding example, `Ticket` would also have the `@Any` qualifier assumed by the container in both declarations.

`@Any` provides us the ability to retrieve all bean instances of a given bean type as it suppresses the addition of the default qualifier by the container.

If we had two beans of the same type, but a different set of qualifiers:

```
@Admin
public class Admin implements Account { ... }

public class User implements Account { ... }
```

We can retrieve all instances of beans that implement `Account` by:

```
@Inject
@Any
Instance<Account> accounts;
```

If we had forgotten to add `@Any` onto the preceding injection point, `@Default` would have been assumed by the container on the injection point and we would only have injected bean instances of type `User`.

Qualifier members

Qualifier annotations are also able to have members defined, which can be used as part of typesafe resolution. If a member is annotated with `@Nonbinding`, it will not be used during typesafe resolution and its value will have no meaning.

If we have the following qualifier annotation with members:

```
@Qualifier
@Retention(RUNTIME)
@Target( { TYPE, METHOD, FIELD, PARAMETER } )
public @interface Book {
  Category value();

  @Nonbinding
  String description() default "";
}
```

We can then create a couple of different implementations such as:

```
@Book(Category.FICTION)
public class FictionSearch implements BookSearch {
}

@Book(value = Category.NONFICTION, description =
"These are nonfiction books.")
public class NonFictionSearch implements BookSearch {
}
```

We can also define an injection point that will inject the `NonFictionSearch` implementation:

```
@Inject
@Book(Category.NONFICTION)
BookSearch search;
```

We can see the impact of `@Nonbinding` by changing `@Book` to the following, and re-deploy the war to an application server with Weld.

```
@Qualifier
@Retention(RUNTIME)
@Target( { TYPE, METHOD, FIELD, PARAMETER } )
public @interface Book {
  @Nonbinding
  Category value();

  @Nonbinding
  String description() default "";
}
```

As opposed to having a `NonFictionSearch` bean injected, we receive a `DeploymentException` exception with the following message:

```
WELD-001409 Ambiguous dependencies for type [BookSearch] with
qualifiers [@Book] at injection point [[field] @Inject @Book
org.cdibook.chapter2.qualifiermembers.Search.search]. Possible
dependencies [[Managed Bean [class
org.cdibook.chapter2.qualifiermembers.FictionSearch] with
qualifiers [@Any @Book], Managed Bean [class
org.cdibook.chapter2.qualifiermembers.NonFictionSearch] with
qualifiers [@Any @Book]]]
```

It might look confusing, but the previous message from Weld is very descriptive about how it informs us that there is more than one bean that is eligible for injection into the `search` field on `Search`.

Alternatives

Alternatives are explicitly declared within `beans.xml` for them to be considered by the container for typesafe resolution, as they are disabled by default. One of the common uses of alternatives is for different deployment scenarios, such as for test deployments.

To create an alternative, a bean only requires the `@Alternative` annotation to be present on its type:

```
@Alternative
@Admin
@User
public class MockAccount implements Account { ... }
```

Activation of the alternative, for beans within the same archive, would need a `beans.xml` with:

```
<beans
  xmlns="http://java.sun.com/xml/ns/javaee"
  xmlns:xsi="http://www.w3.org/2001/XMLSchema-instance"
  xsi:schemaLocation="
  http://java.sun.com/xml/ns/javaee
  http://java.sun.com/xml/ns/javaee/beans_1_0.xsd">

  <alternatives>
    <class>org.cdibook.chapter2.alternatives.MockAccount</class>
  </alternatives>
</beans>
```

If an injection point has ambiguous dependencies during container startup, the container will look for any bean that is an alternative amongst the list of eligible beans. If there is only one alternative bean that is eligible, it will be injected instead of causing a deployment exception.

Resolving Weld deployment errors

Weld will abort the deployment of our application and provide helpful error messages in the server log, when it's unable to identify a single bean for each injection point with typesafe resolution. We would expect to see one or more of unsatisfied or ambiguous dependency errors in this situation.

An unsatisfied dependency occurs when there is not a single bean that is eligible for injection into an injection point. This can be resolved as follows:

- By creating a bean that implements the bean type of the injection point and declares all the qualifier annotations present at the injection point
- If we already have a bean of the correct bean type and all the qualifier annotations in our application, check whether the bean is on the classpath of the bean archive that contains the injection point with the error
- With `beans.xml,` enable an `@Alternative` bean of the correct bean type and qualifier annotations

An ambiguous dependency occurs when there is more than a single bean eligible for injection into an injection point. This can be resolved with the help of the following steps:

1. Add a new @Qualifier to disambiguate between the bean implementations that are eligible for injection.

2. Mark all but one of the bean implementations with @Alternative, thus disabling them by default.

3. Relocate the bean implementations into a separate bean archive that is not on the classpath of the injection point.

4. With beans.xml, disable all but one @Alternative bean that are eligible for injection to that injection point.

 There may be occasions where we do legitimately have an injection point with multiple beans that are eligible. In this instance, we need to use Instance as the bean type of the injection point. We will cover this in the last section of this chapter.

Client proxies

The reference to a bean injected into an injection point, or obtained by programmatic lookup, is usually not a direct reference to an instance of a bean, unless the injected bean is of @Dependent scope.

Instead of the actual bean instance, Weld injects a client proxy that is responsible for ensuring only the bean instance associated with the current context has a method invoked on it. That might sound confusing, but it will become clearer with an example.

```
@RequestScoped
public class RequestBean {
  ...
}

@ApplicationScoped
public class ApplicationBean {
  @Inject
  RequestBean bean;
}
```

Given the two beans we just defined, we would not want the same @RequestScoped bean to be used by all requests to our application, as there is only one instance of the @ApplicationScoped bean. The client proxy is injected into the @ApplicationScoped bean instead of an instance of the @RequestScoped bean and is responsible for retrieving the bean instance from the current request scope whenever a method is called. Through the client proxy, Weld is able to have two different requests using the same @ApplicationScoped bean, while calling methods on their respective @RequestScoped bean instances without us needing to do any special wiring or configuration.

A client proxy is also beneficial in situations where we have a bean in a scope that can be serialized to disk, such as @SessionScoped, and it has references to beans in a scope that can be retrieved at will, such as @ApplicationScoped. It certainly does not provide any benefit to serialize a bean instance that can be retrieved whenever it's needed, so the client proxy is serialized in its place.

> The client proxy being serialized to disk instead of the actual bean instance has the added benefit of not recursively serializing to disk a potentially large tree of bean instances that have references to other beans.

Unproxyable bean types

Due to limitations of the Java language, there are some legal bean types that are not able to have a client proxy created for them by the container. If an injection point tries to inject a bean type that is unable to be proxied, and it is not declared in the @Dependent scope, the container will abort deployment with an appropriate error message.

The following bean types are unable to have a client proxy created for them:

- Classes without a non-private constructor with no parameters, that is, a default constructor
- Classes declared final or with final methods
- Primitive types
- Array types

Here are some tips on how to resolve an unproxyable dependency error, such as the ones just mentioned:

- Add a default constructor to the bean type being injected

- Create an interface that can be implemented by the bean being injected and change the injection point to use the interface instead of the implementation
- If none of the previous work, we can set the scope to be `@Dependent`

Programmatic lookup of contextual instances

We may encounter some situations where it's not convenient to obtain a contextual instance through injection, which are as follows:

- Either the bean type or qualifiers of an injection point may vary at runtime
- In some deployments, there may be no bean that satisfies the bean type and qualifiers of an injection point
- We want to loop through all the beans of a specific bean type

For these situations we obtain an instance of `Instance` parameterized to the bean type we require:

```
@Inject
Instance<BookSearch> bookSearch;
```

To retrieve a contextual instance:

```
BookSearch search = bookSearch.get();
```

We can also alter the bean types that will be retrieved from `Instance` by adding qualifiers either to the injection point or passing them to `select()`.

Specifying qualifiers at the injection is simple:

```
@Inject
@Book(Category.NONFICTION)
Instance<BookSearch> bookSearch;
```

But sometimes it's necessary for the qualifiers to be specified dynamically. For us to use dynamic qualifiers we need to suppress the `@Default` qualifier by specifying `@Any` on the injection point:

```
@Inject
@Any
Instance<BookSearch> bookSearch;
```

Now, we need to create an instance of our annotation `@Book` so it can be passed to `select()`. However, as it's just an interface we aren't able to create one with `new`, we need an implementation of that interface. CDI helps us out by providing `AnnotationLiteral`, a helper class for creating annotation implementations. Our annotation implementation is:

```
public class BookLiteral extends
AnnotationLiteral<Book> implements Book {
  private final Category category;
  private final String description;

  public BookLiteral(Category category, String description) {
    this.category = category;
    this.description = description;
  }

  public Category value() {
    return category;
  }

  public String description() {
    return description;
  }
}
```

So retrieving a bean from `Instance` with a dynamic qualifier is:

```
Annotation qualifier = fiction ? new BookLiteral(Category.FICTION,
"") : new BookLiteral(Category.NONFICTION, "Non Fiction");
BookSearch search = bookSearch.select(qualifier).get();
```

If we had separate qualifiers for fiction and nonfiction books, such as `@NonFiction` and `@Fiction`, instead of `@Book` with a `Category`, we could use dynamic qualifiers without extending `AnnotationLiteral` by creating anonymous classes:

```
bookSearch.select(new AnnotationLiteral<NonFiction>() {}).get();
```

"You can download the example code files for all Packt books you have purchased from your account at http://www.packtpub.com . If you purchased this book elsewhere, you can visit http://www.packtpub.com/support and register to have the files e-mailed directly to you."

Injection point metadata

There is lots of useful metadata information that is present on an injection point, which is represented in the `javax.enterprise.inject.spi.InjectionPoint` interface. Weld provides an implementation of `InjectionPoint` with `@Dependent` scope and `@Default` qualifier for us to retrieve the metadata.

The injection point provides the following functions:

- **getBean()**: This returns the `Bean` object of the bean defined on the injection point

- **getType()**: This returns the bean type of the injection point

- **getQualifiers()**: This returns all the qualifiers of the injection point

- **getMember()**: This returns a different instance depending on whether the injection point utilizes field injection (`Field`), method parameter injection (`Method`), or constructor parameter injection (`Constructor`)

- **getAnnotated()**: This returns `AnnotatedField` for field injection or `AnnotatedParameter` for method and constructor parameter injection

When we have an `@Dependent` scoped bean, there are occasions when it needs to retrieve metadata about the injection point to be properly constructed. A typical example of this requirement is with a logger:

```
class LoggerFactory {
  @Produces
  Logger createLogger(InjectionPoint point) {
    return Logger.getLogger(point.getMember().getDeclaringClass().
getName());
  }
}
```

Injecting a logger with the name set to that of the class is then:

```
@Inject
Logger log;
```

Writing that simple producer has saved us time in not needing to specifically retrieve the class name to set it on a logger in every class we want to use it.

Summary

This chapter explored how dependency injection works with CDI containers through typesafe resolution, to help us understand bean types and qualifiers in determining which bean instance will be injected into an injection point. We covered some built-in qualifiers from the container before we created some of our own qualifiers, with and without members.

Injection points were explained with respect to typesafe resolution, before we looked at the metadata associated with an injection point and how that can be used when creating a bean instance.

We also covered creating alternatives and how they are activated within `beans.xml`, programmatically retrieving a bean instance at runtime for greater control, how Weld uses a proxy for injecting the non `@Dependent` beans, and how to resolve types that cannot be proxied.

3
Deploying JBoss Weld

Now we will cover the installation of **JBoss Weld** into Java EE 6 and Servlet containers. All Java EE 6 containers will come with an implementation of CDI preinstalled, but there may be occasions in which we need to update the version of JBoss Weld that is installed within the container. As a **Servlet container** does not provide a CDI implementation, we will describe the process of installing JBoss Weld into popular Servlet containers.

For this chapter we will use the `chapter3.war`, built from the code of this chapter, to activate JBoss Weld in each container as a way of visualizing the version that has been installed in a container. It's not necessary to use `chapter3.war`, as we can use any WAR file that is CDI-enabled for our purposes.

To build `chapter3.war` for a nonServlet container environment, simply run:

```
mvn clean package
```

JBoss Weld distribution

For installing JBoss Weld into a Servlet container, or updating the version within a Java EE 6 container, we need to download the latest release of Weld 1.1.x from `http://seamframework.org/Weld/Downloads`. Once downloaded, extract the contents of the ZIP file to a local directory such as `C:\Weld`.

 At the time of publication the most recent release of JBoss Weld is 1.1.10.Final.

Taking a look at the contents of `C:\Weld\weld-1.1.10.Final\artifacts\weld`, we can see source and javadoc JARs for the following libraries:

- **weld-api.jar**: These are the extensions to the CDI API

- **weld-core.jar**: This is the JBoss Weld implementation of CDI

- **weld-se.jar**: This is the JAR for Java SE that contains all required classes from CDI and JBoss Weld

- **weld-se-core.jar**: This is the JBoss Weld support for Java SE, which is included within `weld-se.jar`

- **weld-servlet.jar**: This is the JAR for Servlet containers that contains all required classes from CDI and JBoss Weld

- **weld-servlet-core.jar**: This is the core implementation for JBoss Weld in a Servlet container, which is included within `weld-servlet.jar`

- **weld-spi.jar**: This is the service provider interface for containers integrating with JBoss Weld

JBoss AS

JBoss AS7 comes bundled with v1.1.5.Final of JBoss Weld as the default CDI implementation, so we have the choice of using this version with our CDI applications or deciding to upgrade to a more recent version, if available.

When we make the decision to upgrade JBoss Weld, we need to ensure that we are gaining an advantage by doing so, else we could possibly introduce issues into an otherwise stable application server. If our application experiences issues with JBoss Weld that have been resolved in a recent version, upgrading our application server to take advantage of those fixes is definitely a good decision.

If we don't already have it installed, download the latest release of JBoss AS7 from `http://www.jboss.org/jbossas/downloads/` and extract the ZIP contents. We will refer to the location where the ZIP was extracted to as `AS7_HOME`.

 At the time of publication, the most recent binary available for JBoss AS7 is 7.1.1.Final.

With the use of a module system for JBoss AS7, it's very easy for us to upgrade the versions of modules that are installed for all parts of the application server to take advantage of that upgrade.

When we choose to upgrade JBoss Weld from the version within JBoss AS7 to the latest available, provided they are of the same minor version (that is 1.1.x) we can simply update the JAR for the core module as the API and SPI are still the same. The core module for JBoss Weld is located at `AS7_HOME\modules\org\jboss\weld\core\main`.

To update JBoss Weld, we do the following:

1. Copy `weld-core.jar` from `C:\Weld\weld-1.1.10.Final\artifacts\weld` and place it into `AS7_HOME\modules\org\jboss\weld\core\main`.

2. Rename `weld-core.jar` to `weld-core-1.1.10.Final.jar`.

3. Update `module.xml` so that `<resource-root path="">` references the name of the JAR file from Step 2.

 It's not mandatory to perform Step 2, but it does make it quicker to see which version of JBoss Weld is installed in the future.

That's all there is to it! Now we deploy our `chapter3.war` to JBoss AS7, if it isn't already deployed, and start the server.

In the server console during startup we will see messages, like in the following screenshot, which shows that the version of JBoss Weld that was started for `chapter3.war` is 1.1.10.Final:

```
20:31:17,352 INFO  [org.jboss.as.server.deployment] (MSC service thread 1-14) JBAS015876: Starting deployment of "chapter3.war"
20:31:17,603 INFO  [org.jboss.weld.deployer] (MSC service thread 1-7) JBAS016002: Processing weld deployment chapter3.war
20:31:17,688 INFO  [org.jboss.weld.deployer] (MSC service thread 1-14) JBAS016005: Starting Services for CDI deployment: chapter3.war
20:31:17,778 INFO  [org.jboss.weld.Version] (MSC service thread 1-14) WELD-000900 1.1.10 (Final)
20:31:17,827 INFO  [org.jboss.weld.deployer] (MSC service thread 1-12) JBAS016008: Starting weld service for deployment chapter3.war
20:31:18,430 INFO  [javax.enterprise.resource.webcontainer.jsf.config] (MSC service thread 1-15) Initializing Mojarra 2.1.7-jbossorg-1 (20120227-1401) for context '/chapter3'
20:31:19,703 INFO  [org.hibernate.validator.util.Version] (MSC service thread 1-15) Hibernate Validator 4.2.0.Final
20:31:19,880 INFO  [org.jboss.web] (MSC service thread 1-15) JBAS018210: Registering web context: /chapter3
20:31:19,887 INFO  [org.jboss.as] (MSC service thread 1-14) JBAS015951: Admin console listening on http://127.0.0.1:9990
20:31:19,890 INFO  [org.jboss.as] (MSC service thread 1-14) JBAS015874: JBoss AS 7.1.1.Final "Brontes" started in 5476ms - Started 187 of 264 services (76 services are passive or on-demand)
20:31:19,969 INFO  [org.jboss.as.server] (DeploymentScanner-threads - 2) JBAS018559: Deployed "chapter3.war"
```

By opening a browser and navigating to `http://localhost:8080/chapter3/index.jsf`, we can see the result of our simple CDI application as follows:

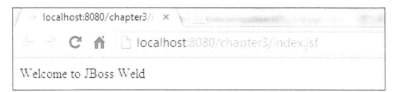

Glassfish

Glassfish comes bundled with JBoss Weld 1.1.8.Final as the default CDI implementation. As with JBoss AS7, we have the choice of using the version that is there already or upgrading to the latest version.

If we don't already have Glassfish installed, download the latest release from `http://glassfish.java.net/public/downloadsindex.html#top` and either run the installation program or extract the contents of the ZIP, depending on our operating system and which installation format we chose. We will refer to the location where we installed Glassfish as `GLASSFISH_HOME`.

 At the time of publication, the most recent download for Glassfish was 3.1.2.2 and is available at `http://glassfish.java.net/downloads/3.1.2.2-final.html`.

As Glassfish uses OSGI bundles for the various pieces that make up the entire server environment, the download of JBoss Weld from earlier does not contain an appropriate JAR that we can use as a replacement for the server.

The appropriate JBoss Weld OSGI bundle, for the most recent release, is available at `https://repository.jboss.org/nexus/content/repositories/releases/org/jboss/weld/weld-osgi-bundle/1.1.10.Final/` and is called `weld-osgi-bundle-1.1.10.Final.jar`.

We need to rename the JAR we just downloaded to `weld-osgi-bundle.jar`, essentially removing all reference to the version of the file, as that is the name of the file we need to replace within Glassfish.

Once renamed, we move `weld-osgi-bundle.jar` into `GLASSFISH_HOME\glassfish\modules` and replace the existing file of that name.

Now we deploy `chapter3.war` to Glassfish by copying it to `GLASSFISH_HOME\glassfish\domains\domain1\autodeploy`.

 The autodeployment directory we just specified refers to `domain1` as the single domain in a default installation, which needs to be modified depending on our environment setup.

And lastly, we run Glassfish using:

```
asadmin start-domain
```

By checking `GLASSFISH_HOME\glassfish\domains\logs\server.log`, we should see an output similar to the following, which informs us that `chapter3.war` was deployed with JBoss Weld 1.1.10.Final:

```
[#|INFO|glassfish3.1.2|org.jboss.weld.Version|_ThreadID=1;_
ThreadName=Thread-2;|WELD-000900 1.1.10 (Final)|#]
```

```
[#|INFO|glassfish3.1.2|javax.enterprise.resource.webcontainer.jsf.
config|_ThreadID=1;_ThreadName=Thread-2;|Initializing Mojarra 2.1.6
(SNAPSHOT 20111206) for context '/chapter3'|#]
```

```
[#|INFO|glassfish3.1.2|javax.enterprise.system.container.web.com.sun.
enterprise.web|_ThreadID=1;_ThreadName=Thread-2;|WEB0671: Loading
application [chapter3] at [/chapter3]|#]
```

```
[#|INFO|glassfish3.1.2|javax.enterprise.system.core.com.sun.enterprise.
v3.server|_ThreadID=1;_ThreadName=Thread-2;|CORE10010: Loading
application chapter3 done in 8,368 ms|#]
```

By opening a browser and navigating to `http://localhost:8080/chapter3/index.jsf`, we will see the message **Welcome to JBoss Weld**.

Apache Tomcat

As **Apache Tomcat** is only a Servlet container, there is no CDI implementation provided by default. This has both an upside and a downside to it. The upside is that we don't have to alter the default configuration and setup of Apache Tomcat in any way to use JBoss Weld with it. The downside is that all of our applications that utilize CDI need to bundle their own copy of JBoss Weld within `WEB-INF/lib` of the WAR.

If we don't already have Apache Tomcat installed, download the latest release from `http://tomcat.apache.org/download-70.cgi` and extract the contents of the ZIP. We will refer to the location where we extracted Apache Tomcat as `CATALINA_HOME`.

 At the time of publication, the most recent download for Apache Tomcat was 7.0.35.

We have a separate Maven profile in our example application for Apache Tomcat that will package `weld-servlet.jar`, along with a JSF implementation, into `WEB-INF/lib` of the archive. The profile also includes `web.xml` so that the servlet listener from JBoss Weld can be used to activate it on startup. The listener definition is as follows:

```
<listener>
  <listener-class>
    org.jboss.weld.environment.servlet.Listener
  </listener-class>
</listener>
```

With our application as it stands, we have JBoss Weld set up to allow us to use the most common development practices of CDI. However, if we need access to the `BeanManager` extension SPI, we need some additional configuration.

JBoss Weld is unable to automatically bind the `BeanManager` extension SPI into JNDI as Apache Tomcat's JNDI is read-only. For the `BeanManager` to be accessible through JNDI, we need to add the following content into `META-INF/context.xml` of our WAR:

```
<Context>
  <Resource name="BeanManager" auth="Container"
    type="javax.enterprise.inject.spi.BeanManager"
    factory="org.jboss.weld.resources.ManagerObjectFactory" />
</Context>
```

Then for the `BeanManager` to be available to our application, we need the following in `web.xml`:

```
<resource-env-ref>
  <resource-env-ref-name>BeanManager</resource-env-ref-name>
  <resource-env-ref-type>
    javax.enterprise.inject.spi.BeanManager
  </resource-env-ref-type>
</resource-env-ref>
```

The `BeanManager` is then accessible from JNDI under `java:comp/env/BeanManager`.

To build `chapter3.war` for Apache Tomcat, we need to run the following command:

```
mvn clean package -PTomcat7
```

Then, copy `chapter3.war` into `CATALINA_HOME\webapps` and run `CATALINA_HOME\bin\startup.bat` or `startup.sh`, depending on your environment.

In the server console, during startup, we will see messages showing that the version of JBoss Weld that was started for `chapter3.war` is 1.1.10.Final, as shown in the following screenshot:

By opening a browser and navigating to `http://localhost:8080/chapter3/index.jsf`, we will see the message **Welcome to JBoss Weld**.

Summary

We've now covered how to upgrade the version of JBoss Weld that is present within a Java EE container, such as JBoss AS7 and Glassfish, as well as how to use JBoss Weld as part of our application on a Servlet container, such as Apache Tomcat.

An important point to note here is how we bundled JBoss Weld into our application and added the servlet listener; they are not specific to Apache Tomcat. Those steps are applicable to all Servlet containers that implement the Servlet 2.5 specification or a more recent version of it.

The only aspect of bundling JBoss Weld for Apache Tomcat that will vary between Servlet containers is how the `BeanManager` extension is attached to JNDI. If a Servlet container has a writable JNDI, JBoss Weld will handle it for us, but if it is a read-only JNDI such as Apache Tomcat, we will need a similar configuration to store the reference into JNDI.

4
Scopes and Contexts

We've already briefly covered scope annotations and how they work, but now we will discuss them in more detail, with emphasis on the conversation scope, followed by pseudo scopes in more detail, and lastly we will provide everything needed to create our own custom scopes.

Scope types

CDI defines two different scope types, **normal scope** and **pseudo scope**, which define how a scope will function within CDI. All the built-in scopes are specified with one of these scope types, and they can also be used to create our own scope, which we will see later in the chapter.

A normal scope is declared with @NormalScope to indicate to the container that a client proxy is required. It has a single attribute, which specifies whether the scope is passivating or not; that is, whether a bean that uses this scope is able to be passivated to secondary storage. @RequestScoped, @SessionScoped, @ApplicationScoped, and @ConversationScoped are all examples of scopes with a normal scope type.

A pseudo scope is declared with @Scope to indicate that no client proxy is required by the container. @Dependent is a scope with a pseudo scope type as instances are never proxied or shared.

Built-in scopes

The term **built-in scope** refers to the scope annotations that are defined by the CDI specification and implemented by Weld for us to use in our applications. They represent the most common scope use cases that are present within web application development in a servlet container. If it didn't provide these scope annotations for us, it would be extremely inefficient and error prone for us to implement our own solutions for these scopes.

The CDI specification defines the following built-in scopes, some of which we've already used in the previous chapters:

- `@RequestScoped`
- `@SessionScoped`
- `@ApplicationScoped`
- `@ConversationScoped`

`@RequestScoped`, `@SessionScoped`, and `@ApplicationScoped` are all applicable to any web application that we develop, and they are accessible from any servlet request within our application.

`@ConversationScoped` is specifically targeted for use with a JSF request by the CDI specification, though it is possible to implement support for other web frameworks by developing a CDI extension. It is available during all lifecycle phases of any JSF faces or a non-faces request. In the next section we will cover this scope annotation in further detail.

 CDI 1.1 will expand `@ConversationScoped` for use with all servlet requests and remove the need for it to be tied to JSF.

Due to CDI's integration with Java EE, the request and application scopes are also active during:

- EJB remote method invocations
- EJB asynchronous method invocations
- EJB timeouts
- Message delivery to a message-driven bean or `MessageListener`
- Web service invocations

Each built-in scope annotation has an associated **context object**, which determines the lifecycle and instance visibility of all beans defined within a given scope. Each built-in scope annotation also has an implementation of the `Context` interface provided by Weld. It is through the `Context` and `Contextual` interfaces that the context implementation works with the Weld container to create and destroy contextual instances.

 A contextual instance is an instance of a bean that was created within a specific context, which is synonymous with it being created in a specific scope.

The request context lifecycle

The request context is the context object for the `@RequestScoped` built-in scope annotation.

It follows the standard pattern of a web request and is activated during any of the following:

- The `service()` method of any servlet
- The `doFilter()` method of any servlet filter
- Calls from the servlet container to any `ServletContextListener`, `HttpSessionListener`, `AsyncListener`, or `ServletRequestListener` listener
- A Java EE web service call
- Asynchronous observer method notification
- EJB remote method invocation, EJB asynchronous method invocation, EJB timeout method call, and EJB message-driven bean message delivery
- Message delivery to a `MessageListener` for a JMS topic or queue, but only if it was obtained from the Java EE component environment

The request context is destroyed at the end of the servlet request and after each of the invocations described previously have completed.

The session context lifecycle

The session context is the context object for the `@SessionScoped` built-in scope annotation. This scope is known as a passivating scope because, depending on the needs of the container, it may need to be serialized to secondary storage for a time, and it needs to implement `Serializable` to support this behavior.

The session context is active during the following:

- The `service()` method of any servlet
- The `doFilter()` method of any servlet filter
- Calls from the servlet container to any `HttpSessionListener`, `AsyncListener`, or `ServletRequestListener`

The session context is shared among all servlet requests that occur within the same HTTPSession.

The session context is destroyed when the following occurs:

- When the HTTPSession times out due to inactivity, but only after all `HttpSessionListener` instances were called

- At the end of any request in which `invalidate()` was called, but only after all filters and `ServletRequestListener` instances were called

The application context lifecycle

The application context is the context object for the `@ApplicationScoped` built-in scope annotation.

The application context is active not only during all the same calls as that of the request context, but also when a disposer method or an `@PreDestroy` method of any bean with any normal scope apart from `@ApplicationScoped` is called.

It is shared between all servlet requests and method calls in which it is active within the same application.

The application context is destroyed when the application that it is associated with is shut down.

The conversation scope

The concept of a conversation will be familiar to those of us that have developed applications with Seam 2. In CDI, the conversation scope is very similar to the session scope, with the main difference being that its activation and deactivation is controlled by our application and not the container.

The conversation scope is also associated with a particular browser tab of a user, unlike the session, which is typically shared between tabs by browsers.

Each conversation is a way to represent a single unit of work that a user will perform to achieve a specific goal or task. As the conversation context holds the state associated with a unit of work by the user, there will be multiple conversations for a single user if they are working on multiple tasks at the same time.

The conversation context lifecycle

The conversation context is the context object for the `@ConversationScoped` built-in scope annotation.

The conversation context is active during any JSF faces or non-faces request.

 The conversation context implementation within Weld was developed to be used specifically with JSF, but it is possible to create an implementation for other web frameworks as well.

Every JSF request is associated with exactly one conversation, which is determined by Weld at the commencement of the JSF restore view phase and is not altered during the entirety of the request.

 In CDI 1.1, the tight coupling with JSF will be removed, enabling the conversation context to be used with other web frameworks.

The default behavior for a conversation, referred to as a **transient conversation**, is for it to be destroyed once a JSF request has completed. However, an application has the ability to promote it to a **long-running conversation** so that it remains active across multiple JSF requests.

Controlling the conversation lifecycle is achieved through a built-in bean that CDI provides just for this purpose:

```
@Inject
Conversation conversation;
```

A transient conversation can be made long-running by calling `conversation.begin()`, and a long-running conversation can be made transient again by calling `conversation.end()`. The following is an example of how we can control conversations:

```
@ConversationScoped
@Stateful
public class AccountRegistration {
    private Account account;

    @Inject
    private Conversation conversation;

    @PersistenceContext(type = EXTENDED)
    EntityManager em;

    @Produces
    public Account getAccount() {
        return account;
    }
```

```
public Account createAccount() {
    account = new Account();
    conversation.begin();
    return account;
}

public void saveAccount(Account account) {
    em.persist(account);
    conversation.end();
}
}
```

The previous example will create a long-running conversation that has a unique identifier assigned to it by Weld, which is used for identifying a conversation and propagating it between requests.

Another option is to explicitly set a unique identifier of our own and pass it to begin() as follows:

```
conversation.begin("MyUniqueId");
```

Conversation propagation

Any long-running conversation that we have created is automatically propagated by Weld between JSF requests with any JSF faces request, resulting from the submission of a JSF form, or redirect. Any non-faces requests, such as a navigation link, will not have a long-running conversation propagated by Weld, but it is possible for us to force this behavior.

As we saw earlier, each long-running conversation has a unique identifier associated with it, which is propagated between JSF requests with the cid request parameter. We can use this parameter force propagation of the long-running conversation with the help of the following code:

```
<h:link outcome="/wizardFinish.xhtml" value="Finish">
    <f:param name="cid" value="#{accountRegistration.conversationId}"
/>
</h:link>
```

 For the previous code snippet to work, we need to add getConversationId() onto the AccountRegistration bean and have it return conversation.getId().

When there are no long-running conversations propagated to a JSF request, then a new transient conversation is created for us. What if we have a long-running conversation but we want to start a new conversation and not have it automatically propagate? We can prevent propagation with the following code:

```
<h:link outcome="newPage.xhtml" value="Start">
    <f:param name="nocid" value="true" />
</h:link>
```

 The `nocid` parameter is specific to Weld, but in CDI 1.1, the specification will include a parameter for this purpose: `conversationPropagation=none`.

Conversation timeout

There are occasions when a long-running conversation cannot be restored and associated with a new request. They are usually due to the following:

- HTTP servlet session invalidation
- Weld destroying it if it is not associated with a current JSF request, for the purposes of conserving resources

In the latter situation, we are able to provide a hint to Weld as to whether it's possible that a long-running conversation is likely to be used after a period of activity by setting a timeout as follows:

```
conversation.setTimeout(milliseconds);
```

 There is nothing in the CDI specification that mandates a container to adhere to any timeout set on a conversation; it is only meant as a hint as to whether it may be likely to be used again.

Pseudo scopes

Pseudo scopes result in beans that do not have a client proxy created by Weld, but instead a new instance is created each time and the client holds a direct reference to it. `@Dependent` is a scope annotation that is a pseudo scope type, and `@Dependent` is also the default scope for any beans that do not explicitly declare a scope.

Beans with a scope of @Dependent are never shared; it is a dependent object of whichever object it was injected into. This means that the @Dependent bean is created at the point when the object it belongs to is created, and is destroyed when the object it belongs to is destroyed.

> Accessing a @Dependent bean by its EL name will cause a new instance of that bean to be created every time the expression is evaluated, which can be several times when using JSF. For this reason, it is not recommended to use @Dependent beans in EL expressions as it is likely that the desired behavior will not be achieved; instead, add the @Dependent bean to a normal scope bean and use a getter to retrieve the @Dependent bean from it.

Custom scopes

Creating a custom scope is usually the preserve of framework developers, but it can be beneficial for us to understand how they can be created as we may find the need to write one in the future.

To create a new pseudo scope we use the following code:

```
@Scope
@Retention(RUNTIME)
@Target( { METHOD, TYPE, FIELD } )
public @interface MyPseudoScope {}
```

But as it is unlikely that we will need to create a pseudo scope, the following is how to create a new normal scope:

```
@NormalScope
@Retention(RUNTIME)
@Target( { METHOD, TYPE, FIELD } )
public @interface MyNonPassivatingScope {}
```

As the default value for the passivating attribute on @NormalScope is false, we don't need to set it if we want to define a non-passivation capable scope.

Either of these scopes could then be used just as any other of the built-in scopes provided in CDI by annotating a bean with the scope annotation.

Creating the scope is the easy part; the difficult task is to implement a Context interface for the new scope. The Context interface provides operations for obtaining contextual instances with a particular scope of any contextual type by calling operations of Contextual.

Our application doesn't need to call the `Context` interface directly, but it will be called by Weld and maybe by CDI extensions. We will discuss how a CDI extension can be developed in *Chapter 8, Writing a Portable Extension.*

```
public interface Context {
    public Class<? extends Annotation> getScope();
    boolean isActive();
    public <T> T get(Contextual<T> bean);
    public <T> T get(Contextual<T> bean, CreationalContext<T>
creationalContext);
}
```

Creating an implementation of `Context` for `@MyNonPassivatingScope` would mean the following:

* `getScope()` returns `MyNonPassivatingScope .class`.
* `isActive()` will return true only when the context object is active with respect to the current thread.
* `get()` obtains contextual instances of the contextual type represented by the instance of `Contextual`. If `isActive()` is false, we must throw a `ContextNotActiveException` exception. Both forms of `get()` will return an existing instance if found, but if one isn't found it will return the following:
    ◦ `null` if no `CreationalContext` is given or if `Contextual.create()` returns `null`
    ◦ A newly created instance of the contextual type if a `CreationalContext` is provided

For Weld to know about our implementation of `Context`, we need to register it with the container. We can do that within a CDI extension by observing the `AfterBeanDiscovery` event from Weld, as shown in the following code snippet:

```
public MyExtension implements Extension {
    void afterBeanDiscovery(@Observes AfterBeanDiscovery event,
BeanManager manager) {
        event.addContext(new MyNonPassivatingScopeContext());
    }
}
```

The implementation of a `Context` object is a difficult task, which is why the example implementation in the code for this chapter has only implemented the methods in a way that enables the `Context` object to be registered with Weld.

Summary

We've now learned in greater detail about scopes and contexts, and how they relate to each other. The lifecycles for the request, session, and application scopes were explained with regards to how they relate to the lifecycle of a web container, with a detailed explanation of the conversation scope for JSF.

Normal and pseudo scopes were differentiated, and we talked about `@Dependent`, which is a built-in pseudo scope.

Lastly, we showed how framework developers can create their own scope and context for CDI, for their own or everyone's applications.

5
Producers

In this chapter we will expand on producers, which were introduced back in *Chapter 1, What is a Bean?*, by covering their uses in greater detail. We will also see what scopes our produced beans are in and how to ensure that the beans we produce don't leave pieces of themselves behind when they're destroyed.

We've already learned how producers can be useful when we want to make runtime decisions about which bean instance should be used in a given situation. But there can be many situations where producers are beneficial, such as enabling third-party frameworks to be used with CDI by exposing their objects as beans.

Producers allow us to utilize runtime polymorphism, such as:

```
@SessionScoped
public class SearchManager implements java.io.Serializable {

  private SearchType searchType= SearchType.FICTION;

  @Produces
  @Preferred
  public BookSearch getSearch() {
    switch (searchType) {
      case FICTION:
        return new FictionSearch();
      case NONFICTION:
        return new NonFictionSearch();
      default:
        return null;
    }
  }
```

An injection point matching the bean we just produced is as follows:

```
@Inject
@Preferred
BookSearch search;
```

The scope of a producer

Beans created by a producer defaults to be `@Dependent` scoped. A producer with no scope specified will be called each and every time Weld needs to inject a bean that is matched by the producer's bean types and qualifiers. It also means there will be a separate instance of the bean for each call made to the producer, which is not always what we want or intend.

CDI makes it easy for us to modify this behavior by adding any of `@RequestScoped`, `@ConversationScoped`, `@SessionScoped`, or `@ApplicationScoped` onto the producer, depending on which lifecycle we want for the produced bean. If we were to annotate a producer with `@ApplicationScoped`, the producer would only be called once for the life of the application, and the created bean is stored in the application context to be shared by all clients.

 A producer does *not* derive its scope from the bean in which it is declared.

An important point to remember when thinking of producers is that they are themselves a bean in their own right, even though they may be a field or method of another bean. It's for this reason that a producer does not derive its scope from the bean it is contained within, as CDI treats the producer as a separate bean, and if it requires a scope then it must be specified on the producer.

Injection into producer methods

Coming back to our producer method at the start of the chapter, there is one problem that we may experience as the code is currently written. Creating `FictionSearch` and `NonFictionSearch` with the Java `new` operator means that they are not eligible for dependency injection and cannot have interceptors.

Both of those restrictions may be acceptable to our application, but if they aren't then we can use dependency injection into the producer method to ensure that we are using beans controlled by Weld. The producer would now be as follows:

```
@Produces
@Preferred
```

```
@SessionScoped
public BookSearch getSearch(FictionSearch fs, NonFictionSearch nfs) {

  switch (searchType) {
    case FICTION:
      return fs;
    case NONFICTION:
      return nfs;
    default:
      return null;
  }
}
```

In our example, `FictionSearch` and `NonFictionSearch` are both `@RequestScoped` beans; so what does that mean for our producer as we're producing a bean into `@SessionScoped`? Our producer method has the effect of promoting the request scope instance into the session scope, which is probably not what we intended to happen.

We can see the effect of that promotion when we create a simple JSF app with two pages, and each page outputs the description of two beans defined by these injection points:

```
@Inject
FictionSearch fictionSearch;

@Inject
@Preferred
BookSearch search;
```

We've seen the second injection point before; it receives the bean instance from our producer and the first is just a direct injection of the `FictionSearch` instance from the request scope.

To be able to compare direct injection of the request-scoped `FictionSearch` and the session-scoped `BookSearch`, we need to make a minor change to our producer to update the description:

```
case FICTION:
  fs.setDescription("Hello from Fiction Search!");
  return fs;
```

This small change allows us to see a different description for the bean instance that was returned from our producer and the request scoped instance.

Deploying our application and accessing `http://localhost:8080/chapter5/index.jsf`, we see the following screen:

We can see that the request scope and session scope beans have different descriptions associated with them, as we expected after modifying our producer method.

What is probably not expected is that when we click on **Next Request** or refresh the same page, we see the following screen:

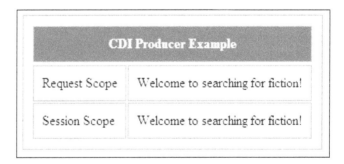

What happened there? As soon as our producer had a bean from the request scope injected into it, which we then promoted to the session scope, that bean instance was destroyed at the end of the request. Instead of retaining the bean with the modified description between requests, what we retrieve from the session scope is actually the new bean instance from the request scope as our producer is not called again. That is why we see the same description for the bean in two different scopes; they are both retrieving the description from the same requestscoped bean instance.

There are several ways to resolve this unintended behavior:

- Change the scope on FictionSearch and NonFictionSearch, but that would result in changes to all places where these beans are used, which we may not want to do

- Change the scope of our producer to @Dependent or @RequestScoped, which doesn't do us any good if we want the produced bean to live longer

- Use the @New qualifier, which will be covered in the next section

Dependent beans for producers

In creating a new bean with a producer, there may be situations in which we do not want an existing instance of a bean to be injected into our producer, but would prefer an instance that is dependent on the scope of the bean that produced it.

Taking our example from the previous section, we can resolve the problem of a requestscoped bean being promoted to the session scope with the following producer:

```
@Produces
@Preferred
@SessionScoped
public BookSearch getSearch
(@New FictionSearch fs, @New NonFictionSearch nfs) {

  switch (searchType) {
    case FICTION:
      fs.setDescription("Hello from Fiction Search!");
      return fs;
    case NONFICTION:
      return nfs;
    default:
      return null;
  }
}
```

Deploying our example and accessing `http://localhost:8080/chapter5/index.jsf`, we see the same initial screen as shown previously. If we now refresh the page or click on **Next Request**, we see that the session-scoped bean has been retained as we originally intended:

 Whatever scope a bean type has declared on it, injecting an instance of that bean type with `@New` will always provide a bean that is dependent on where it was injected.

Using `@New` on the parameters of the producer allows Weld to inject a new dependent instance of `FictionSearch` and `NonFictionSearch` that will be bound into the session context. These dependent objects won't be destroyed until `SearchManager` is removed when the user session expires.

 CDI 1.1 will deprecate the use of `@New` in favor of using `@Dependent` to the injection point to signify the need for a dependent instance of a bean type.

Cleanup of produced beans

Often, the producers we create produce a bean that either requires explicit destruction or closure, or another object may need to be destroyed once the bean that was using it is no longer required.

For these situations, CDI provides a means by which we can perform a customized cleanup within our application by creating a disposer method to match the producer.

```
public class AccountDatabase {

  @Produces
  @ConversationScoped
  @AccountDB
  public EntityManager create(EntityManagerFactory factory) {
```

```
      return factory.createEntityManager();
    }

    public void close(@Disposes @AccountDB EntityManager em) {
      em.close();
    }
  }
```

A disposer method is required to have a single parameter annotated with `@Disposes` that has the same bean type and qualifiers as the producer. When a disposer method declares additional parameters, these are treated as injection points by Weld, allowing us to inject loggers or other beans that are needed to perform the cleanup process.

 A disposer method must reside within the same bean class as the producer that created the bean instance being cleaned up.

For a given producer, there can only be one disposer method that matches the bean type and qualifiers, otherwise Weld will cease deployment of the application and log the error. Conversely, it is entirely fine for a single disposer method to be matched with more than one producer, which makes it convenient for cleaning up beans of a similar type in a single method.

Taking our earlier example, we can extend it for multiple producers with a single disposer:

```
public class Databases {

  @Produces
  @ConversationScoped
  @AccountDB
  public EntityManager accountDB(EntityManagerFactory factory) {
    return factory.createEntityManager();
  }

  @Produces
  @ConversationScoped
  @OrderDB
  public EntityManager orderDB(EntityManagerFactory factory) {
    return factory.createEntityManager();
   }

  public void close(@Disposes @Any EntityManager em) {
    em.close();
  }
}
```

Summary

We now have a complete understanding of producers and their various aspects within CDI development for our applications. We covered what scope is assigned to a bean instance created from a producer and how to inject instances of beans into our producers; so that we may create producers that take advantage of runtime decision making about the exact bean instance that needs to be returned. We also learnt how to prevent unintended scope problems of bean instances being used in a producer by requesting a dependent instance from Weld with @New and creating a method to clean up any resources that may remain open when a bean instance is destroyed by Weld.

6
Interceptors and Decorators

This chapter will cover how interceptors and decorators can be utilized within our CDI applications, while doing so in a typesafe manner through annotations. We will examine how interceptor bindings are created through annotations and then how to create and enable an interceptor. In decorators, we talk about what a delegate is before enabling decorators in a manner similar to interceptors.

Interceptors and decorators behave as two different sides of the same coin. Interceptors are perfect for separating concerns that are orthogonal to our application purpose by cutting across all layers of our application to perform an identical task. These tasks usually relate to technical matters such as transaction management, security, and method logging.

As interceptors are not aware of the semantics of what they intercept, they are not suited for separating business concerns, but that's where decorators come into play. As decorators intercept methods on a specific interface, they know everything about the context in which that interface is used. Decorators are well suited for solving business problems that apply to a hierarchy of classes of the same type. In most cases, it would be possible to implement the same functionality as a decorator within an abstract parent of these classes, but then we lose the ability to disable and enable that functionality as required.

Interceptor bindings

If we want to provide auditing in our application, such as a sequence of particular events that occur, then we can use interceptors to help us. First off, we need to define an interceptor binding type that we can use to inform Weld about which beans we want to audit:

```
@InterceptorBinding
@Target( { METHOD, TYPE } )
@Retention( RUNTIME )
public @interface Audited {}
```

With the interceptor binding type created, we can set our `AccountManagement` to be an audited bean:

```
@Audited
public class AccountManagement { ... }
```

Though, if we only want a specific method to be audited, we can specify:

```
public class AccountManagement {
  @Audited
  public void createAccount() { ... }
}
```

Creating and enabling an interceptor

Now that we have the interceptor binding type, we need to implement the interceptor. All that's required is to create a standard interceptor and annotate it with `@Interceptor` and our interceptor binding type of `@Audited`:

```
@Audited
@Interceptor
public class AuditInterceptor {
  @AroundInvoke
  public Object auditMethod(InvocationContext ctx)
  throws Exception
  { ... }
}
```

CDI interceptors are also able to take full advantage of dependency injection like all beans in our application:

```
@Audited
@Interceptor
public class AuditInterceptor {

  @Inject
  AuditService service;

  @AroundInvoke
  public Object auditMethod(InvocationContext ctx)
  throws Exception
  { ... }
}
```

Now we're ready to enable our interceptor for our application. As all interceptors are disabled by default, we need to enable our interceptor within the `beans.xml` file of a bean archive:

```
<beans
  xmlns="http://java.sun.com/xml/ns/javaee"
  xmlns:xsi="http://www.w3.org/2001/XMLSchema-instance"
  xsi:schemaLocation="
    http://java.sun.com/xml/ns/javaee
    http://java.sun.com/xml/ns/javaee/beans_1_0.xsd">
  <interceptors>
    <class>org.cdibook.chapter6.AuditInterceptor</class>
  </interceptors>
</beans>
```

 Activation of an interceptor within `beans.xml` will activate it for all beans within the same archive only.

It might seem strange to be using XML with a framework that espouses annotations over an XML configuration, but it does provide the following advantages that wouldn't be possible otherwise:

- We can specify an absolute ordering of all interceptors within our application to ensure deterministic behavior and startup.
- Our interceptor can be enabled or disabled during deployment. So we can only enable our auditing interceptor in production and not in development and test environments.

 The interceptor's ordering is determined by the order of the `<class>` elements within `beans.xml`.

Advanced interceptors

These next sections will delve deeper into interceptor binding types to explain more advanced use cases of them. We will cover binding types with members, how to combine different interceptors for a single use, and how binding types can be inherited.

Interceptor binding types with members

Just as with qualifier annotations, we can also add members to interceptor binding types too, such as:

```
@InterceptorBinding
@Target( { METHOD, TYPE } )
@Retention( RUNTIME )
public @interface Audited {
  boolean logToFile() default false;
}
```

With the binding type we just created, we need to create a new interceptor that matches the situation of logToFile being true, as CDI uses the member as a means for choosing a different interceptor implementation. For our preceding interceptor binding type, the implementation would be:

```
@Audited( logToFile = true )
@Interceptor
public class AuditFileInterceptor {
  @AroundInvoke
  public Object auditMethod(InvocationContext ctx)
  throws Exception
  { ... }
}
```

And we would use the interceptor with a member:

```
@Audited( logToFile = true )
public class AccountManagement { ... }
```

What if we don't necessarily need to create two separate interceptors, and we're using logToFile as a way to pass information into our interceptor and not to provide a completely separate interceptor implementation? In this situation, we can retain the original interceptor implementation and use the @Nonbinding annotation on the member of the binding type:

```
@InterceptorBinding
@Target( { METHOD, TYPE } )
@Retention( RUNTIME )
public @interface Audited {
  @Nonbinding
  boolean logToFile() default false;
}
```

Combining interceptor binding types

Binding two separate interceptors to a bean is only a matter of adding their binding type annotations to the bean itself. However, we may encounter a complicated use case that requires a separate interceptor to handle the combination of the two binding types. For this situation, the interceptor itself can specify multiple bindings:

```
@Audited
@Loggable
@Interceptor
public class AuditLoggingInterceptor { ... }
```

We can bind our interceptor to the `createAccount()` method with any of these combinations:

```
public class AccountManagement {
  @Audited
  @Loggable
  public void createAccount() { ... }
}
```

Or:

```
@Audited
@Loggable
public class AccountManagement {
  public void createAccount() { ... }
}
```

Or:

```
@Audited
public class AccountManagement {
  @Loggable
  public void createAccount() { ... }
}
```

This previous example could also have the annotations reversed between the type and method, as both will achieve the same result.

Inheritance of interceptor binding types

We are able to implement inheritance within interceptor binding types as their definition is transitive.

 An interceptor binding type that is annotated with another interceptor binding type allows the former binding type to inherit the latter.

```
@Loggable
@Audited
@InterceptorBinding
@Target( { METHOD, TYPE } )
@Retention( RUNTIME )
public @interface AuditLogged {}
```

This removes the need to use both `@Loggable` and `@Audited` on a bean type or method. To ensure that both interceptors are called, we can simply annotate it with `@AuditLogged` to achieve the same result.

 If our `AuditLoggingInterceptor` exists within the system and is enabled, it would also be called along with the interceptors for `@Loggable` and `@Audited`.

What is a decorator delegate?

Say our application has beans that implement the following:

```
public interface Account {
  Account create();
  String getId();
  void changePassword(String password);
}
```

We want to monitor how frequently the password on an account is changed to track potential hacking in our system. A decorator is an ideal way to solve the problem.

Our decorator is a bean, which can be abstract, that implements the required type and is annotated with `@Decorator`:

```
@Decorator
public abstract class PasswordMonitorDecorator implements Account {
  @Inject
  @Delegate
  @Any
```

```
  Account account;

  @PersistenceContext
  EntityManager em;

  public void changePassword(String password) {
    account.changePassword(password);
    em.persist(new PasswordChange(account.getId()));
  }
}
```

As the decorator can be abstract, we only need to implement the methods of the type being decorated if our decorator needs to perform any special operations when that method is called.

 If a method has both interceptors and decorators, interceptors are called first.

In our decorator, the **account** field is known as the delegate injection point of the decorator. As we specified @Any, the decorator will be bound to all beans that implement Account. If we didn't need or want all of the beans that implement Account to be bound to the decorator, we can utilize qualifiers on the delegate injection point to restrict the set of beans that match.

 A decorator may call any method that is present on the delegate object, not just the method being decorated.

Enabling a decorator

As with interceptors, all decorators are disabled by default, so we need to enable our decorator within the beans.xml file of a bean archive:

```
<beans
  xmlns="http://java.sun.com/xml/ns/javaee"
  xmlns:xsi="http://www.w3.org/2001/XMLSchema-instance"
  xsi:schemaLocation="
    http://java.sun.com/xml/ns/javaee
    http://java.sun.com/xml/ns/javaee/beans_1_0.xsd">
  <decorators>
        <class>org.cdibook.chapter6.PasswordMonitorDecorator</class>
  </decorators>
</beans>
```

Activation of a decorator within `beans.xml` will activate it for all beans within the same archive only.

Summary

In this chapter, we introduced the use of interceptors and decorators in CDI, including how they are enabled within `beans.xml` of a bean archive.

For interceptors, we explained what a binding type was and how it supported inheritance. We also covered how to use binding and `@Nonbinding` members of an interceptor binding type, and how different interceptor binding types can be combined on bean types and methods.

We saw a situation in which a decorator is suited to solve a business problem, how to specify that a class implementing a bean type is a decorator, and what delegate object is injected into the decorator.

7
Events

We're now going to find out about events within CDI, such as how they are fired, how we listen for new events, what we can use as an event payload, and how we can narrow what events we can listen to and fire. All of these we will discover while staying within the boundaries of typesafe Java, making our runtime less error-prone.

Events may be produced and consumed by beans of our application, but there is absolutely no coupling between the bean producing an event and the one consuming it. This allows our beans to interact without any coupling or compile-time dependencies between them.

What is a payload?

The payload of an event, the event object, carries any necessary state from the producer to the consumer and is nothing but an instance of a Java class.

 An event object may not contain a type variable, such as <T>.

We can assign qualifiers to an event and thus distinguish an event from other events of an event object type. These qualifiers act like selectors, narrowing the set of events that will be observed for an event object type.

There is no distinction between a qualifier of a bean type and that of an event, as they are both defined with @Qualifier. This commonality provides a distinct advantage when using qualifiers to distinguish between bean types, as those same qualifiers can be used to distinguish between events where those bean types are the event objects.

An event qualifier is shown here:

```
@Qualifier
@Target ( { FIELD, PARAMETER } )
@Retention ( RUNTIME )
public @interface Removed {}
```

How do I listen for an event?

An event is consumed by an **observer method**, and we inform Weld that our method is used to observe an event by annotating a parameter of the method, the **event parameter**, with @Observes. The type of event parameter is the event type we want to observe, and we may specify qualifiers on the event parameter to narrow what events we want to observe.

We may have an observer method for all events produced about a Book event type, as follows:

```
public void onBookEvent(@Observes Book book) { ... }
```

Or we may choose to only observe when a Book is removed, as follows:

```
public void onBookRemoval(@Observes @Removed Book book) { ... }
```

 Any additional parameters on an observer method are treated as injection points.

An observer method will receive an event to consume if:

- The observer method is present on a bean that is enabled within our application
- The event object is assignable to the event parameter type of the observer method

How do I fire an event?

We fire events with an instance of the parameterized Event interface, which can be obtained through injection as follows:

```
@Inject
Event<Book> bookEvent;
```

We then fire the event using the following:

```
bookEvent.fire(book);
```

This event can be consumed by any observer method that matches the event object type and does not specify additional qualifiers. In our case, that would be the first observer method from the previous section.

 If an exception is thrown within an observer method, Weld stops further calls to matching observer methods and the exception is rethrown by `fire()`.

Event qualifiers

When we want to specify qualifiers on an event we intend to fire, there are two ways it can be achieved:

- Annotating the `Event` injection point with qualifiers
- Passing qualifiers to the `select()` method of `Event` dynamically

As we've seen in previous examples, specifying qualifiers at an injection point is easy.

```
@Inject
@Removed
Event<Book> bookRemovedEvent;
```

Every call to `bookRemovedEvent.fire()` will have the event qualifier `@Removed` and would match the second observer method we defined earlier in the chapter.

The downside of specifying event qualifiers on the injection point, as just done, is that we are not able to specify event qualifiers dynamically. We can modify our previous `Event` injection point to the following:

```
@Inject
@Any
Event<Book> bookRemovedEvent;
```

And instead set the qualifier dynamically by using this:

```
bookEvent
  .select( new AnnotationLiteral<Removed>(){} )
  .fire(book);
```

The `AnnotationLiteral` class is a helper class provided by CDI to make it easier for us to obtain a qualifier instance without having to create concrete classes.

 Event qualifiers can comprise a combination of annotations at the Event injection point and qualifier instances passed to `select()`.

Members of event qualifiers

As with other qualifiers, we're able to add members to our event qualifiers that can either be part of differentiating qualifier instances or just for providing additional information.

```
@Qualifier
@Target( { PARAMETER, FIELD } )
@Retention( RUNTIME )
public @interface Book {
  BookType value();
}
```

Say we fire an event as follows:

```
public void addBook(Book book) {
  bookEvent
    .select(new BookLiteral(book.getBookType()))
    .fire(book);
}
```

To complete the preceding code, we need to create a `BookLiteral` class using the CDI `AnnotationLiteral` helper class.

```
public abstract class BookLiteral
  extends AnnotationLiteral<Book>
  implements Book {

  private BookType type;

  public BookLiteral(BookType type) {
    this.type = type;
  }

  public BookType value() {
    return type;
  }
}
```

We could have also created an empty `BookLiteral` implementation and overridden `value()` within our call to `select()`, but the preceding approach ensures we aren't repeating code by firing the same event and event qualifier somewhere else within our applications.

In such cases, we can then listen to these events with observer methods as follows:

```
public void fictionBookAdded(@Observes @Book(FICTION) Book book) {
    ...
}

public void nonFictionBookAdded(@Observes @Book(NONFICTION)
    Book book) {
    ...
}
```

Instead of using `BookLiteral` to dynamically set the event qualifiers when firing the event, we could have specified them on the injection point as follows:

```
@Inject
@Book(FICTION)
Event<Book> bookEvent;
```

 Event qualifier members can be marked with `@Nonbinding` to prevent them from being a part of the process of matching observer methods to fired events.

Combining event qualifiers

Just as with qualifiers, we can combine any number of event qualifiers either on an injection point, by dynamically setting them on the event, or a combination of both approaches.

```
@Inject
@Book(FICTION)
Event<Book> bookEvent;
...
bookEvent.select(new AnnotationLiteral<Added>(){}).fire(book);
```

To have an observer method notified when the preceding event is fired, it needs to match all event qualifiers associated with the event when it was fired. If we're missing just one event qualifier, or a member of an event qualifier has a different value, our observer method will not be called as we expected.

Say we have observer methods such as the following:

```
public void afterFictionBookAdded(@Observes @Book(FICTION)
  @Added Book book) { ... }

public void afterBookAdded(@Observes @Added Book book) { ... }

public void onBookEvent(@Observes Book book) { ... }
```

In such cases, only `afterFictionBookAdded()` will be called as it matches the fired event with `@Added` and `@Book(FICTION)`.

Now say we had an observer method such as the following:

```
public void afterAdding(@Observes @Any Book book) { ... }
```

The preceding observer method would also be notified, as `@Any` informs Weld that we want to be notified of all `Book` events, irrespective of what event qualifiers may be set.

Observing events in different transaction phases

If an observer method wishes to receive events as part of the before or after completion phases of a transaction in which the event was fired, they are referred to as **transactional observer methods**.

We could incorporate the transaction phase into our preceding observer with the following:

```
public void refreshOnBookRemoval
  (@Observes( during = AFTER_SUCCESS ) @Removed Book bk) { ... }
```

The possible values for `during` are defined on `javax.enterprise.event. TransactionPhase`. In the context of a transactional observer method, the values for `TransactionPhase` have the following meanings:

- `IN_PROGRESS`: An observer method is called immediately. As this is the default value for all observers, there is no need to set it if the standard behavior is required.

- `BEFORE_COMPLETION`: An observer method is triggered during the before completion phase of the transaction.

- `AFTER_COMPLETION`: An observer method is triggered during the after completion phase of the transaction.

- AFTER_SUCCESS: In the same phase of the transaction as AFTER_COMPLETION, but only if the transaction completes successfully.

- AFTER_FAILURE: In the same phase of the transaction as AFTER_COMPLETION, but only if the transaction fails to complete successfully.

Although AFTER_COMPLETION, AFTER_SUCCESS, and AFTER_FAILURE all result in an observer method being called at the same point in the transaction lifecycle, it can be advantageous to distinguish between whether the transaction completed, completed successfully, or failed.

 If there is no transaction in progress when an event is fired, a transactional observer method receives the event at the same time as other observer methods. It acts as though the during member of @Observes had not been set.

Now that we've learned about transactional observer methods, it's time to see how useful they can be! When our application utilizes a stateful object model, and we have state that is maintained for longer than a single transaction, we want the ability to update that long-held state without refreshing an entire set of objects through additional database calls.

For a bookstore application, we may want to retain a list of books that are currently available for purchase, but we don't want to retrieve that data for every user request as it changes infrequently. We need an applicationscoped bean to retain the list of books.

```
@ApplicationScoped
@Singleton
public class BookCatalog {
  @PersistenceContext
  EntityManager em;

  List<Book> books;

  @Produces
  @Available
  public List<Book> getAvailableBooks() {
    if (null == books) {
      books = em.createQuery
      ("select b from Book b where b.archived = false")
      .getResultList();
    }
    return books;
  }
}
```

Say we have a bean that raises an event when it adds a new `Book` element:

```
bookEvent.select(new AnnotationLiteral<Added>(){}).fire(book);
```

And when it removes a `Book` element:

```
bookEvent.select(new AnnotationLiteral<Removed>(){}).fire(book);
```

In such cases, we can modify `BookCatalog` to update the list of available books when it receives the events for adding and removing books, as follows:

```
public void addBook(@Observes(during = AFTER_SUCCESS)
  @Added Book book) {
  books.add(book);
}

public void removeBook(@Observes(during = AFTER_SUCCESS)
  @Removed Book book) {
  books.remove(book);
}
```

Event-observer bean creation

When Weld is in the process of delivering events to observers during our call to `Event.fire()`, it will automatically instantiate the bean that defines the observer method to be called if there isn't currently an instance of that bean present within the current context.

For most cases that is perfectly fine, but there may be situations where that default behavior is unwanted. Thankfully, CDI allows us to define a **conditional observer**, such that the bean will only observe events if it's already present within the current context.

We can specify a conditional observer by setting a value for the `notifyObserver` member of `@Observes`.

```
public void refreshOnBookRemoval
  (@Observes( notifyObserver = IF_EXISTS ) @Removed Book bk)
  { ... }
```

Any bean in the scope of @Dependent is not allowed to be a conditional observer, as there would be no way for the bean to be instantiated and observe the event.

The possible values for notifyObserver are defined in javax.enterprise.event.Reception. Apart from IF_EXISTS, the only other option is ALWAYS, which is the default.

Summary

We discussed some of the advantages of decoupling our application beans by using event producers and consumers. We then looked at what constitutes an event payload and how to define an event qualifier. Using event qualifiers and @Observes, we created observer methods to consume events that were produced with a call to Event.fire().

We expanded on event qualifiers to cover how to use qualifier members with events and the different approaches for combining multiple event qualifiers when firing and observing events. We also saw how events can be observed based on different phases of the transaction lifecycle, and whether a transaction was successfully completed or not.

Lastly, we looked at how a bean with an observer method is automatically instantiated, if it isn't already present in the current context, and how to prevent that instantiation if it is not desired.

8
Writing a Portable Extension

As CDI was never intended to be a stationary target, only being enhanced and updated as part of a JSR, a series of **SPIs (Service Provider Interfaces)** are exposed by CDI so that developers like us can extend and enhance CDI through portable extensions.

We'll look at how to create a portable extension, what is the container lifecycle and how it can be utilized in creating additional functionality in CDI, how we can consume CDI beans from non-CDI beans, and some example extensions to provide an idea of what can be achieved.

What is a portable extension?

A portable extension is a Java Service Provider that is retrieved during container startup by Weld and notified at each stage of the container lifecycle, based on which events our portable extension needs to observe.

What a portable extension can achieve within CDI is only limited by our imagination and the current SPI that is available in a particular release!

As stated in the specification:

A portable extension may integrate with the container by:

- *Providing its own beans, interceptors, and decorators to the container*
- *Injecting dependencies into its own objects using the dependency injection service*
- *Providing a context implementation for a custom scope*
- *Augmenting or overriding the annotation-based metadata with metadata from some other source*

To create a portable extension, we only need to complete two steps:

1. Write a Java class that implements `javax.enterprise.inject.spi.Extension` as follows:

   ```
   public class OurExtension implements Extension { ... }
   ```

2. Register the extension as a service provider by creating `META-INF/services/javax.enterprise.inject.spi.Extension` and setting the content of the file to the classname of our extension:

   ```
   org.cdibook.chapter8.OurExtension
   ```

 Although an extension is not a CDI bean, it can be injected into any bean after the Weld initialization process has completed, just like any other bean.

A single instance of our extension is maintained by Weld for the lifetime of our application, so it is possible to interact with our extension from within our application as if it was `@ApplicationScoped`.

What is the CDI container lifecycle?

When an application is initialized, Weld fires an event at each stage of the container lifecycle that allows extensions to integrate with the initialization process of Weld.

The container lifecycle consists of the following event sequence:

1. The `BeforeBeanDiscovery` event is fired before Weld begins the process of discovering beans within our application. This event allows us to add scopes, annotated types, qualifiers, stereotypes, and interceptor bindings to our application. Adding an annotated type is the most powerful, as this allows us to take a class that would not be a bean and make it a bean within our application.

2. The `AfterBeanDiscovery` event is fired by Weld when it has fully completed the bean discovery process and verified that there are no definition errors with the beans that were discovered within our application. Our extension can observe this event to add new beans, observer methods, or context.

3. The `AfterDeploymentValidation` event is fired by Weld after verifying that there are no deployment problems, but before it creates any contexts or processes a request. Our extension can use this event to add a validation error that we are aware of, maybe through a custom bean of ours (causing Weld to abort deployment) or we can remove any temporary storage we may have created as part of previous events that is no longer required.

4. The `BeforeShutdown` event will be fired by Weld once it has finished processing all requests and destroyed all contexts.

Each of these events is fired once by Weld for our application as part of the container lifecycle.

Between `BeforeBeanDiscovery` and `AfterBeanDiscovery`, Weld fires the following events based on what was found in our bean archive during its scanning:

- The `ProcessAnnotatedType` event is fired for each type that is present within the bean archive. This occurs prior to the annotations on the type being read, allowing us to prevent the type from being used, and thus prevent any further initialization processing of it, or replace the `AnnotatedType`.

- The `ProcessInjectionTarget` event is fired for every bean and Java EE component, such as a servlet or Session Bean, that is the target of an injection point within our application.

- The `ProcessBean` event is fired for every bean, interceptor, or decorator within a bean archive, as long as the bean is not annotated with `@New`. The type of bean that was discovered by Weld will determine which one among `ProcessManagedBean`, `ProcessSessionBean`, `ProcessProducerMethod`, and `ProcessProducerField` is fired.

- The `ProcessProducer` event is fired for each producer, method, or field that is present on an enabled bean of our application.

- The `ProcessObserverMethod` event is fired for each observer method that is present on an enabled bean of our application.

 Any `AnnotatedType` that was added to Weld during the `BeforeBeanDiscovery` event will not have a `ProcessAnnotatedType` event fired for it. This will be fixed as part of CDI 1.1 in such a way that a `ProcessAnnotatedType` event is fired.

Here's a simple example of our extension modifying the metamodel by preventing a bean from being enabled, and thus present within our application, if it is annotated with `@Disable`:

```
public class OurExtension extends Extension {

  public <T> void processAnnotatedType(
    @Observes ProcessAnnotatedType<T> type) {

    if (type.getAnnotatedType().isAnnotationPresent
```

```
        (Disable.class)) {
        type.veto();
      }
    }
  }
}
```

If our extension needs to make use of the `BeanManager` when observing an event, it can be injected as follows:

```
public <T> void processAnnotatedType(
  @Observes ProcessAnnotatedType<T> type,
  BeanManager beanManager) {
  ...
}
```

BeanManager

The core piece in extending CDI with extensions is the `BeanManager`, as it provides programmatic access to a CDI container via an API. `BeanManager` provides many useful operations for developers writing an extension, some of which include the ability to obtain beans, interceptors, decorators, observers, and contexts.

Accessing the `BeanManager` is not restricted to injection into extension observer methods; we are able to inject it into any bean or other Java EE component that supports injection.

```
@Inject
BeanManager beanManager;
```

 There is no restriction on when the `BeanManager` methods can be called during the life of an application.

Injection into non-container managed instances

Sometimes we have a class that has CDI injection point on it but it isn't instantiated by the container, so it is not available for injection to be performed on it. An example of this is a portlet class that needs to inject beans into itself, but a portlet class is instantiated and controlled by a portlet container so Weld is unable to perform injection on it.

In our example, the portlet class would be classified as a **non-container managed instance**, as the instance of the portlet class is not created by Weld and therefore not managed by it either.

We can ask Weld to perform injection on our portlet class instance as follows:

```
// get the BeanManager, from JNDI in this example
BeanManager beanManager = (BeanManager)
  new InitialContext().lookup("java:comp/BeanManager");

// create an AnnotatedType for our class
AnnotatedType<MyPortlet> portletType =
    beanManager.createAnnotatedType(myPortlet.getClass());

// create an InjectionTarget
InjectionTarget<MyPortlet> injectionTarget =
    beanManager.createInjectionTarget(portletType);

// create the CreationalContext that is required for each instance
CreationalContext ctx = beanManager.createCreationalContext(null);

// call initializer methods and perform injection on our myPortlet
// instance
injectionTarget.inject(myPortlet, ctx);

// call @PostConstruct
injectionTarget.postConstruct(myPortlet);
```

You may have noticed that we didn't call `injectionTarget.produce()` in our example. In this case, we already had an instance of our class that required injection to be performed, so we did not need to create a new instance of the class within Weld.

We can then clean up the objects in our example by using the following:

```
// Call @PreDestroy on our class
injectionTarget.preDestroy(myPortlet);

// Discard the instance
injectionTarget.dispose(myPortlet);

// Clean up the CreationalContext
ctx.release();
```

This example shows how we can perform injection into a portlet class that is managed by a portlet container, but the same principles apply to injecting beans into a third-party framework class too.

The main change that would be required is calling the following:

```
ThirdPartyComponent instance = injectionTarget.produce(ctx);
```

This will construct an instance of the `ThirdPartyComponent` class that is now managed by Weld.

Registering a bean

An extremely common use case for extension developers is to register one or more beans with Weld to make them available within an application. To make it possible to register new beans, CDI provides the `Bean` interface, which represents a bean within an application. For every bean in our application, including interceptors, decorators, and producers, there is an instance of `Bean` that is registered with the `BeanManager`.

 The `AnnotatedType` represents the metadata of a bean type, which is used by Weld to then construct a physical `Bean` instance from that metadata.

We will create a simplified example of how an extension can add a bean to a CDI application.

```
public class AddBeanExtension implements Extension {

  public void afterBeanDiscovery
    (@Observes AfterBeanDiscovery after, BeanManager beanMgr) {

    // read the annotations of our class
    AnnotatedType<MyClass> type =
      beanMgr.createAnnotatedType(MyClass.class);

    // instantiate class and inject dependencies
    final InjectionTarget<MyClass> injectionTgt =
      beanMgr.createInjectionTarget(type);

    after.addBean( new Bean<MyClass>() { ... } );
  }
}
```

Replacing annotations on a type via an extension

Assume we have an application that was written with plain POJOs but we want to migrate to CDI. If our POJOs already have a home-grown annotation, possibly for documentation purposes in the past, we can use that annotation as a stepping stone to CDI annotations.

Say our application currently has the following annotation defined, and it's used on all POJOs:

```
@Retention(RUNTIME)
@Target(TYPE)
public @interface PojoDoc {
   String value();
   ScopeEnum scope() default ScopeEnum.REQUEST;
}
```

Our application has the following two beans, as an example:

```
@PojoDoc("myRequestBean")
public class MyRequestBean { ... }

@PojoDoc(value = "userSession", scope = ScopeEnum.SESSION)
public class MySessionBean implements Serializable { ... }
```

And we have a new CDI bean that we want to use them in:

```
@RequestScoped
public class UsageBean {
   @Inject
   MyRequestBean requestBean;

   @Inject
   MySessionBean sessionBean;
}
```

As it currently stands, both `requestBean` and `sessionBean` will be dependent scoped instances. What if we want CDI to treat them as `@PojoDoc` defines them? We can achieve it with the following extension:

```
public class PojoDocExtension implements Extension {

   <X> void processType(@Observes ProcessAnnotatedType<X> event) {

      AnnotatedType<X> orig = event.getAnnotatedType();
```

```
        if (orig.isAnnotationPresent(PojoDoc.class)) {

          Annotation scopeAnnotation = null;
          PojoDoc pojoDoc = orig.getAnnotation(PojoDoc.class);

          switch (pojoDoc.scope()) {
            case REQUEST:
              scopeAnnotation = new RequestScopedLiteral();
              break;
            case SESSION:
              scopeAnnotation = new SessionScopeLiteral();
              break;
            case APPLICATION:
              scopeAnnotation = new ApplicationScopedLiteral();
              break;
          }

          AnnotatedType<X> updated = new AnnotatedTypeBuilder<X>()
            .readFromType(orig, true)
            .addToClass(
            new NamedLiteral(pojoDoc.value())
            )
            .addToClass(scopeAnnotation)
            .removeFromClass(PojoDoc.class)
            .create();

          event.setAnnotatedType(updated);
        }
      }
    }
```

What our extension does is listen for the ProcessAnnotatedType event and look for types that have an annotation of @PojoDoc set on them, as these will be our POJOs that are not specifically built for CDI.

We use the scope() value within the @PojoDoc instance from the type to determine whether we need to add a scope annotation for @RequestScoped, @SessionScoped, or @ApplicationScoped. This behavior is all handled within the switch statement.

Finally, we create a new `AnnotatedType` with the help of the `AnnotatedTypeBuilde` class from **Apache DeltaSpike**, by adding the scope annotation we created and `@Named` with the value retrieved from the `@PojoDoc` value. We also removed the `@PojoDoc` annotation from our bean, as it has no meaning for Weld, though we could just as easily have left it there. The new `AnnotatedType` we created is then set back onto the event, replacing the type that we received on the event so ours will be used to define the metadata for the bean instead.

For this example, we utilized Apache DeltaSpike for working with the `AnnotatedType` instances to make our work a bit simpler.

 At the time of publication, the latest Apache DeltaSpike release was 0.3-incubating.

Summary

We've barely scratched the surface of portable extensions in this chapter, as there are an enormous number of things that can be achieved when utilizing the CDI container lifecycle. So many, in fact, that this is one of those rare situations where your imagination is more likely to be an inhibiting factor, and not the available SPI of CDI.

We explained what a portable extension is and what is required of us in developing one and having Weld recognize it. We briefly went through the CDI container lifecycle, discussing the events that are fired by Weld at each phase, while providing some ideas about what can be done as part of each event. We looked at the `BeanManager`, a core part of any extension developer's toolkit, before we learned how to perform injection into an instance that is not managed by Weld. Then we showed how a new bean can be created and registered with Weld using the `Bean` interface.

At the end of the chapter, we showed a complete example of an extension that took an existing annotation from non-CDI designed POJOs and converted it into several CDI-specific annotations to provide the originally anticipated behavior within CDI.

Our example extension provides a good starting point for writing more complex extensions while also providing insight into what can be done. For instance, we could use the idea in our example to replace annotations or metadata on the POJOs of a framework to enable them as CDI beans.

9
Book Store – CDI Services

This chapter will explore creating parts of a real-life application with CDI to provide a more indicative picture of how it can be utilized. We will also cover some of the CDI usage patterns that can be beneficial for us to include in our applications as they are developed. Parts of the application will provide clear examples of topics that we have discussed in the previous chapters, while providing a means to see how a particular topic that we covered can be integrated into an application.

Overview of the application

The application that we will build with CDI is one that we will all be familiar with, that of an online book store! Though we don't intend to develop the application to the level of complexity that is provided by `Amazon.com`, it will provide a good overview of using CDI within an application for us to explore various aspects of its development.

The entities our application will require are as follows:

- `User`: This entity will hold the user login credentials, and is applicable to customers and internal site administrators.

- `Account`: This entity is used for capturing additional information that only applies to customers, such as addresses, and it will be the link to any orders that a customer may place.

- `Category`: This entity defines a grouping that a book is part of.

- `Author`: This entity specifies an author within the application that can be linked to a book.

- `Book`: This entity captures all the information about a particular book, and links to the category and author associated with it.

- `Order`: This entity captures all the information about an order placed by a customer account. It will link to one or more `OrderItem` entities that will capture which book is being ordered and in what quantity.

Adding interceptors for our services

Before we begin developing our services, as part of the design process, we decided that we wanted to restrict access to some methods based on the `User` role and that some methods would require a `Transaction` object to be present.

Securing methods with an interceptor

To be able to develop an interceptor that we can use in our services, there are a few pieces that must be created, as shown in the following list:

1. We need to define an `enum` function for the possible roles using the following code:

```
public enum RoleType {
    GUEST,
    USER,
    ORDER_PROCESSOR,
    ADMIN;
}
```

2. We also need an annotation that we can add to methods to inform CDI that we want them to be intercepted:

```
@InterceptorBinding

@Target( { TYPE, METHOD } )

@Retention( RUNTIME )
public @interface Secure {

    @Nonbinding
    RoleType[] rolesAllowed() default {};
}
```

 We specified the `RoleType` as `@Nonbinding` as its value is only important to the interceptor implementation and nothing else.

Within our interceptor, we need to know whether there is currently a user logged into the application, and what his/her `RoleType` is; otherwise, we will not be able to determine whether we should grant him/her access to the method!

3. We will create a CDI bean that we can use to hold the information about the current user, as follows:

```
public class CurrentUser implements Serializable {
```

```
private boolean loggedIn = false;
private Long userId;
private String name;

private String email;
private RoleType roleType = RoleType.GUEST;
public CurrentUser() {
}
public CurrentUser(Long id, String name, String email,
RoleType roleType) {
    this.userId = id;
    this.name = name;
    this.email = email;
    this.loggedIn = true;
    this.roleType = roleType;
}
public Long getUserId() {
    return userId;
}
public String getName() {
    return name;
}
public String getEmail() {
    return email;
}
public boolean isLoggedIn() {
    return loggedIn;
}
public RoleType getRoleType() {
    return roleType;
}
}
```

We've made `CurrentUser` implement `Serializable` as we will be injecting this bean into a `@SessionScoped` bean later.

 At present, this bean will always return `false` when `isLoggedIn()` is called, and `GUEST` when `getRoleType()` is called. This is intentional as when we discuss services later, we will discover how we can update them.

4. To make it easier to distinguish between possible instances of `CurrentUser` within our application, we will introduce a qualifier that we can use:

```
@Qualifier
@Target( { FIELD, PARAMETER, METHOD } )
@Retention( RUNTIME )
public @interface LoggedIn {}
```

5. Now that we have all the pieces, we can create our interceptor for securing our service methods as follows:

```
@Secure

@Interceptor
public class SecurityInterceptor {

    @Inject

    @LoggedIn
    Instance<CurrentUser> currentUserInstance;

    @AroundInvoke
    public Object checkRoles(InvocationContext context) throws
Exception {
        // Check for defined roles
        Secure secure = getAnnotation(context.getMethod());
        RoleType[] roles = secure.rolesAllowed();
        if (roles.length == 0) {
            throwException("No RoleType's defined for @Secure: ",
context.getMethod());
        }
        boolean roleMatches = false;
        for (int i = 0; i < roles.length; i++) {
            if (roles[i].equals(currentUserInstance.get().
getRoleType())) {
                roleMatches = true;
                break;
            }
        }
        if (!roleMatches) {
            throwException("User does not have permission to call
method: ", context.getMethod());
        }
        return context.proceed();
    }
    ...
}
```

 We injected `Instance<CurrentUser>` instead of `CurrentUser` to ensure that at the point the interceptor is called, we are retrieving the most recent `CurrentUser`, instead of the one that was present when the interceptor was created, which could possibly be different.

Inside `checkRoles()`, we retrieve the `@Secure` annotation from the method or class depending on where it was defined, to know what roles are allowed for this method call. If the `RoleType` value on `CurrentUser` matches one of the allowed roles, then we call `context.proceed()`; otherwise we throw an `AuthorizationException`.

Providing a transaction with an interceptor

We also need an interceptor for ensuring that particular service calls are present within a `UserTransaction` of the container. We will use the following steps to do so:

1. The annotation for the transaction doesn't require any values, so it is just as follows:

```
@InterceptorBinding

@Target( { TYPE, METHOD } )

@Retention( RUNTIME )
public @interface Transactional {}
```

2. And our interceptor utilizes an injected `UserTransaction` to determine whether we're already associated with a transaction, or we need to begin one as shown in the following code snippet:

```
@Transactional

@Interceptor
public class TransactionInterceptor {

  @Resource
  UserTransaction userTrans;

  @AroundInvoke
  public Object manageTransaction(InvocationContext context)
throws Exception {
    boolean transactionPresent = false;
    if (userTrans.getStatus() == Status.STATUS_NO_TRANSACTION) {
      userTrans.begin();
    } else {
      transactionPresent = true;
    }
    Object result;
    try {
      result = context.proceed();
    } catch (Exception e) {
```

```
            userTrans.rollback();
            throw e;
        }
        if (userTrans.getStatus() == Status.STATUS_MARKED_ROLLBACK) {
            userTrans.rollback();
        } else if (userTrans.getStatus() != Status.STATUS_ROLLEDBACK)
{

            if (!transactionPresent) {
              userTrans.commit();
            }
        }
        return result;
    }
}
```

3. To activate our two interceptors within the application, we need to include them into the beans.xml file of our archive, which is located in META-INF of our jar:

```
<beans xmlns="http://java.sun.com/xml/ns/javaee"
xmlns:xsi="http://www.w3.org/2001/XMLSchema-instance"
        xsi:schemaLocation="http://java.sun.com/xml/ns/javaee
http://java.sun.com/xml/ns/javaee/beans_1_0.xsd">
    <interceptors>
      <class>
        org.cdibook.chapter9.interceptor.SecurityInterceptor
      </class>
      <class>
        org.cdibook.chapter9.interceptor.TransactionInterceptor
      </class>
    </interceptors>
</beans>
```

We deliberately chose to list SecurityInterceptor before TransactionInterceptor; the order in beans.xml determines the order in which they are executed, as there is no need to start a transaction if the caller does not have the necessary permissions to execute the method.

Creating CDI services

In creating the services that interact with JPA, we decided to abstract some methods out into a parent service that all our services can inherit. It wasn't necessary to develop it in this way, as it is all down to personal preference in the end.

1. Our parent service will inject an `EntityManager` for JPA calls, and will take advantage of **Java Generics** to provide some common methods for retrieving an entity by an identifier and retrieving all instances of an entity type:

```java
public abstract class AbstractService<T> {

  @Inject

  @BookDB
  private EntityManager entityManager;
  private Class<T> entityClass;
  public AbstractService() {}
  public AbstractService(Class<T> entityClass) {
    this.entityClass = entityClass;
  }
  protected EntityManager getEntityManager() {
    return entityManager;
  }

  @Transactional
  public T get(Long id) throws ServiceException {
    ...
  }

  @Transactional
  public List<T> getAll(Map<String, String> parameters) {
    ...
  }
  protected Predicate[] buildPredicates(Map<String, String>
params, CriteriaBuilder criteriaBuilder, Root<T> root) {
    return new Predicate[]{};
  }
}
```

We use `@Transactional` on `get()` and `getAll()` to indicate that we wish those methods to be called with an active transaction, as the annotation will trigger our interceptor to be called, but only when it has been defined within `beans.xml`, as we did earlier.

 The implementation of `get()` and `getAll()` utilize JPA criteria-building APIs, and can be seen within the code of the chapter.

2. Now that we've created the abstract service, let's create a service to manage `User` data:

```java
@RequestScoped
public class UserService extends AbstractService<User> {
  ...
  @Transactional

  @Secure(rolesAllowed = {RoleType.GUEST, RoleType.ADMIN})
  public void createUser(User user) throws ServiceException {
    if (null != user.getId()) {
      throw new EntityExistsException();
    }
    try {
      getEntityManager().persist(user);
    } catch (ConstraintViolationException cve) {
      throw new ServiceException(cve);
    }
  }

  @Secure(rolesAllowed = RoleType.GUEST)
  public void login(String email, String password) throws
ServiceException {
    if (currentUserInstance.get().isLoggedIn()) {
      // Already logged in
      return;
    }
    Map<String, String> params = new HashMap<>();
    params.put("email", email);
    List<User> results = getAll(params);
    if (null == results||results.size() == 0||results.size() > 1)
{
      throw new ServiceException("User record not found.");
    }
    User user = results.get(0);
    if (!user.passwordMatches(password)) {
      throw new ServiceException("Unable to login user.");
    }
    userLoggedInEvent.fire(user);
  }
  ...
}
```

Currently we've defined `UserService` as `@RequestScoped`, as there is no reason to make it live for longer than that with the current design. We've added `@Transactional` and `@Secure` onto our methods, restricting `login()` to only be called when the `RoleType` value is `GUEST` and `createUser()` is restricted to `GUEST` and `ADMIN`. It might seem unusual for `createUser()` to be restricted in such a way, but it does make sense for our application as we want to restrict the ability to create a user in the application to new customers and administrators.

> The `ConstraintViolationException` is wrapped into our application's `ServiceException` because it is not `Serializable`, which prevents it from being used as a test exception scenario with **Arquillian** — the integration testing framework from JBoss.

3. As part of `login()`, we fire a CDI event to inform any part of our application that is listening that there is now a non `GUEST` user accessing the application. As shown in the following code, we need to provide a means for a `CurrentUser` entity to be produced by our application that does not contain the default values, as we saw earlier:

```
@SessionScoped
public class Authentication implements Serializable {
private CurrentUser currentUser;
  public void userLoggedIn(

    @Observes(notifyObserver = Reception.IF_EXISTS)
              @LoggedIn User loggedInUser) {

  currentUser = new CurrentUser(loggedInUser.getId(),
                                loggedInUser.getName(),
                                loggedInUser.getEmail(),
                                loggedInUser.getRoleType());
  }
  public void userLoggedOut(

    @Observes(notifyObserver = Reception.IF_EXISTS)
              @LoggedOut CurrentUser currentUser) {
    if (null != this.currentUser
        && this.currentUser.equals(currentUser)) {
      this.currentUser = null;
    }
  }
}
```

```
@Produces

@Named("currentUser")

@LoggedIn
public CurrentUser produceCurrentUser() {
    return null != this.currentUser ? this.currentUser : new
CurrentUser();
    }
}
```

Our `@SessionScoped` bean stores a non CDI managed instance of `CurrentUser`, which is created when it observes the `@LoggedIn` event from `UserService.login()`. For any other part of our application that needs to inject `CurrentUser`, our bean defines a producer that provides a `@Dependent` scoped instance to whichever `InjectionPoint` requires it. Though the produced bean is cleaned up whenever the bean it was injected into goes out of scope, the bean that produced it will remain in the session until it expires.

4. Taking a brief look at `AccountService`, we can see the aggregation of business method calls as `AccountService` utilizes `UserService` to create a user for an account:

```
@RequestScoped
public class AccountService extends AbstractService<Account> {

    @Inject
    UserService userService;
    public AccountService() {
        super(Account.class);
    }

    @Transactional

    @Secure(rolesAllowed = RoleType.GUEST)
    public void register(Account account) throws ServiceException {
        if (null == account.getUser()) {
            throw new IllegalArgumentException("User can not be null on
Account");
        }
        if (null != account.getId()) {
            throw new EntityExistsException();
        }
        userService.createUser(account.getUser());
        try {
```

```
        getEntityManager().persist(account);
    } catch (ConstraintViolationException cve) {
        throw new ServiceException(cve);
    }
  }
}
```

Summary

Development of the services, interceptors, and events for our book store application has put into practice all that we have learned in the previous chapters. The chapter included only snippets of the most important code that is available, but there is also code for other services, and all the JPA entity classes with their relationships.

Looking at the code for the chapter, there are also several integration tests for the services that utilize Arquillian to perform in-container testing with JBoss AS7.

10
Book Store – User Interfaces

This chapter will expand the book store application we developed the services for in *Chapter 9*, *Book Store – CDI Services*, by developing a user interface for the customer and administrator using two different technologies. This will enable us to see how CDI services can be reused to create two distinct user interfaces.

The customer user interface will be developed with **AngularJS**, though it could have been developed with any other JavaScript or view technology currently available. It will interact with CDI through REST to retrieve and store the data as required.

The administration interface will instead be developed with **JSF2** and **RichFaces** for additional components for our interface. We will develop CDI beans for use in the JSF views to interact with our services, as we deem necessary.

 AngularJS information can be found at http://angularjs.org/.

REST services

To enable us to access our CDI services from AngularJS, we need to expose them over REST, though the use of REST is just one of the many choices that could have been made.

For retrieving books from our database, we need a REST service similar to the following:

```
@Path("/books")
public class BookListResource {

    @Inject

    BookService bookService;
```

```
    @GET

    @Produces(MediaType.APPLICATION_JSON)
    public List<Book> getAvailableBooks() {
        List<Book> results = bookService.getAvailableBooks();
        Collections.sort(results, new BookTitleSorter());
        return results;
    }

    @GET

    @Path("/{categoryId}")

    @Produces(MediaType.APPLICATION_JSON)
    public List<Book> getAvailableBooksByCategory(@
PathParam("categoryId") long categoryId) {
        Map<String, String> params = new HashMap<>();
        params.put("available", "true");
        params.put("categoryId", Long.toString(categoryId));
        List<Book> results = bookService.getAll(params);
        Collections.sort(results, new BookTitleSorter());
        return results;
    }
}
```

Most of the annotations are related to configuring how the REST endpoints will be exposed and under which paths, but we can see that utilizing our CDI service is only two lines of code to inject it. Then it's available for any of our methods on this REST implementation.

To retrieve a single book, given its ID—such as when selecting a book from a list to see more details—we need the following code:

```
@Path("/book")
public class BookResource {

    @Inject
    BookService bookService;

    @GET

    @Path("/{bookId}")

    @Produces(MediaType.APPLICATION_JSON)
    public Book getBook(@PathParam("bookId") Long bookId) {
        try {
            return bookService.get(bookId);
```

```
        } catch (ServiceException e) {
            return null;
        }
    }
}
```

And when we need to interact with our `UserService` and `AccountService`, we need the following REST endpoint:

```
@Path("/account")
public class AccountResource {

    @Inject

    @LoggedIn
    Instance<CurrentUser> currentUserInstance;

    @Inject
    AccountService accountService;

    @Inject
    UserService userService;

    @GET

    @Produces(MediaType.APPLICATION_JSON)
    public CurrentUser getCurrentUser() {
        return currentUserInstance.get();
    }

    @POST

    @Path("/register")

    @Consumes(MediaType.APPLICATION_JSON)

    @Produces(MediaType.APPLICATION_JSON)
    public RestResult register(GuestUser guestUser) {
        User user = new User(guestUser.getName(), guestUser.
getEmail(), RoleType.USER, guestUser.getPassword());
        Account acct = new Account(user);
        RestResult result = new RestResult();
        try {
            accountService.register(acct);
            result.setSuccess(true);
        } catch (ServiceException e) {
            result.setSuccess(false);
        }
```

```
            return result;
        }
        @POST

        @Path("/login")

        @Consumes(MediaType.APPLICATION_JSON)

        @Produces(MediaType.APPLICATION_JSON)
        public RestResult login(GuestUser guestUser) {
            RestResult result = new RestResult();
            try {
                userService.login(guestUser.getEmail(), guestUser.
getPassword());
                result.setSuccess(true);
            } catch (ServiceException e) {
                result.setSuccess(false);
            }
            return result;
        }

        @GET

        @Path("/logout")
        public void logout() {
            userService.logout();
        }
}
```

 We inject the CurrentUser entity into the endpoint in order to use it when we need to retrieve the details of the logged-in user.

User interface for customers

Now that we have the REST endpoints in place, we are now able to call them from AngularJS! To create a service for login, logout, and register, it only needs to interact with $resource, from AngularJS, to call the REST endpoints as shown in the following code:

```
angular.module('user.services', ['ngResource']).
    service('User', function ($resource) {
        var loadUser = function (success) {
            $resource('/chapter10/rest/account').get(function
(userData) {
                if (userData.userId) {
                    if (success) {
```

```
                              success(userData);
                  }
              }
          });
    };
    this.register = function (user, success, error) {
        $resource('/chapter10/rest/account/register').save(user,
function (response) {
              if (response.success) {
                  success();
              } else {
                  error();
              }
        }, error);
    };
    this.login = function (user, success, error) {
        $resource('/chapter10/rest/account/login').save({
              email : user.email,
              password : user.password
        }, function (response) {
              if (response.success) {
                  loadUser(success);
              } else {
                  error();
              }
        }, error);
    };
    this.logout = function () {
        $resource('/chapter10/rest/account/logout').get();
    };
  });
```

Our registration page that uses the REST endpoint looks like the following screenshot:

Administration interface

To enable an administrator to login to the site, we need a CDI bean that JSF can use in the page, as shown in the following code:

```
@Named("login")

@RequestScoped
public class LoginBean {
    private String email;
    private String password;

    @Inject
    UserService userService;
    public String getEmail() {
        return email;
    }
    public void setEmail(String email) {
        this.email = email;
    }
    public String getPassword() {
        return password;
    }
    public void setPassword(String password) {
        this.password = password;
    }
    public void submit() throws ServiceException {
        userService.login(email, password);
    }
}
```

This bean will capture the login credentials and perform the `login` operation on `UserService`. The following is the JSF view that will be used for logging in:

```
<rich:panel>
  <f:facet name="header">
    <h:outputText value="Login" />
  </f:facet>
  <h:form>
    <h:panelGrid columns="2">
      <h:outputText value="Email: " />
      <rich:inplaceInput defaultLabel="click to enter your email"
value="#{login.email}" />
      <h:outputText value="Password: " />
      <rich:inplaceInput defaultLabel="click to enter your password"
value="#{login.password}" />
```

```
        </h:panelGrid>
        <h:commandButton value="Login" action="#{login.submit}" />
    </h:form>
</rich:panel>
```

The bean used to retrieve the current users present in the database is very basic, as shown in the following code:

```
@Named("users")

@ViewScoped
public class UsersBean implements Serializable {

    @Inject
    UserService userService;
    public List<User> getAllUsers() {
        return userService.getAll(null);
    }
}
```

 Given how basic this method call to our service is, we could easily have marked `UserService` with `@Named` and used it directly within our JSF page. At the moment that would not have caused any issues with the REST services using the service, but that may not be the case as development continues. Sometimes it is best to keep a separation between the service and how it is used by a view technology.

To display the users on our page we would use the following code:

```
<rich:tabPanel switchType="client">
    <rich:tab header="Users">
        <rich:dataTable value="#{users.allUsers}" var="user">
            <rich:column>
                <f:facet name="header">Name</f:facet>
                <h:outputText value="#{user.name}" />
            </rich:column>
            <rich:column>
                <f:facet name="header">Email</f:facet>
                <h:outputText value="#{user.email}" />
            </rich:column>
        </rich:dataTable>
    </rich:tab>
</rich:tabPanel>
```

This would look like the following screenshot:

Summary

Though brief, and far from being a complete application, we've seen in this chapter how quickly we can connect our CDI services to AngularJS or JSF. This makes it extremely easy to take advantage of whichever technology we prefer for our development, or it might be the newest that we want to try.

Index

Symbols

runtime polymorphism, utilizing 47
scope 48
producer method
about 17
injecting into 48-50
pseudo scope
about 37, 43
creating 44

Q

qualifier
@Any qualifier 19
@Default qualifier 19
about 9, 10, 18
members 20, 21

R

request context
lifecycle 39
REST service 95, 96
RichFaces 95
administration interface, developing 95
runtime polymorphism
utilizing 47

S

scope
about 10
types 37
scope, types
normal scope 37
pseudo scope 37
scope() value 80
search field 21
select() method 25, 65, 66
service() method 39
Service Provider Interfaces. *See* SPI
Servlet container
about 29
JBoss Weld, installing 29
ServletRequestListener instance 40
Session Beans 12
session context
destroying 40
lifecycle 39

SPI 73
switch statement 80

T

ThirdPartyComponent class 78
transaction
providing, with an interceptor 87, 88
transactional observer methods 68
Transaction object 84
TransactionPhase
AFTER_COMPLETION transaction 68
AFTER_FAILURE transaction 69
AFTER_SUCCESS transaction 69
BEFORE_COMPLETION transaction 68
IN_PROGRESS transaction 68
transient conversation 41
typesafe resolution
about 17
advantages 18

U

unproxyable bean type 24
User entity 83
user interface
about 95
developing, with AngularJS 95
for customers 98, 99
REST services 95, 96
UserService.login() 92
UserTransaction method 87

V

value() 67

W

weld-api.jar 30
weld-core.jar 30
Weld deployment errors
resolving 22
weld-se-core.jar 30
weld-se.jar 30
weld-servlet-core.jar 30
weld-servlet.jar 30
weld-spi.jar 30

Thank you for buying
JBoss Weld CDI for Java Platform

About Packt Publishing

Packt, pronounced 'packed', published its first book "*Mastering phpMyAdmin for Effective MySQL Management*" in April 2004 and subsequently continued to specialize in publishing highly focused books on specific technologies and solutions.

Our books and publications share the experiences of your fellow IT professionals in adapting and customizing today's systems, applications, and frameworks. Our solution based books give you the knowledge and power to customize the software and technologies you're using to get the job done. Packt books are more specific and less general than the IT books you have seen in the past. Our unique business model allows us to bring you more focused information, giving you more of what you need to know, and less of what you don't.

Packt is a modern, yet unique publishing company, which focuses on producing quality, cutting-edge books for communities of developers, administrators, and newbies alike. For more information, please visit our website: www.packtpub.com.

About Packt Open Source

In 2010, Packt launched two new brands, Packt Open Source and Packt Enterprise, in order to continue its focus on specialization. This book is part of the Packt Open Source brand, home to books published on software built around Open Source licences, and offering information to anybody from advanced developers to budding web designers. The Open Source brand also runs Packt's Open Source Royalty Scheme, by which Packt gives a royalty to each Open Source project about whose software a book is sold.

Writing for Packt

We welcome all inquiries from people who are interested in authoring. Book proposals should be sent to author@packtpub.com. If your book idea is still at an early stage and you would like to discuss it first before writing a formal book proposal, contact us; one of our commissioning editors will get in touch with you.

We're not just looking for published authors; if you have strong technical skills but no writing experience, our experienced editors can help you develop a writing career, or simply get some additional reward for your expertise.

JBoss AS 7 Configuration, Deployment and Administration

ISBN: 978-1-84951-678-5   Paperback: 380 pages

Build a fully-functional, effecient application sever using JBoss AS

1. Covers all JBoss AS 7 administration topics in a concise, practical, and understandable manner, along with detailed explanations and lots of screenshots

2. Uncover the advanced features of JBoss AS, including High Availability and clustering, integration with other frameworks, and creating complex AS domain configurations

3. Discover the new features of JBoss AS 7, which has made quite a departure from previous versions

JBoss ESB Beginner's Guide

ISBN: 978-1-84951-658-7   Paperback: 320 pages

A comprehensive, practical guid to developing service-based application using the Open Source JBoss Enterprise Service Bus

1. Maximize the use of Spring features in Python and develop impressive Spring Python applications

2. Explore the versatility of Spring Python by integrating it with frameworks, libraries, and tools

3. Discover the non-intrusive Spring way of wiring together Python components

Please check **www.PacktPub.com** for information on our titles

Drools JBoss Rules 5.X Developer's Guide

ISBN: 978-1-78216-126-4   Paperback: 338 pages

Define and execute your business rules with Drools

1. Learn the power of Drools as a platform for writing your business rules

2. Integrate Drools into your Java business application using the Spring framework

3. Through real-world examples and solutions, you will be taken from novice to expert

Instant Drools Starter

ISBN: 978-1-78216-554-5   Paperback: 52 pages

The ultimate Starter guide for ecaluatinf rules engines and getting started with Drools

1. Learn something new in an Instant! A short, fast, focused guide delivering immediate results.

2. Discover Drools and learn to harvest the power of rules

3. Write a rules engine and put it into practice

4. Explore key features from brass tacks syntax to testing and troubleshooting

Please check **www.PacktPub.com** for information on our titles

www.ingramcontent.com/pod-product-compliance
Lightning Source LLC
Chambersburg PA
CBHW060155060326
40690CB00018B/4127